AGAINST THE ODDS

Six Projects

and Letters to the Six Intrepid Colleagues-in-Arms

Who Helped to Change Small Pieces of the World

Belden Paulson

Thistlefield Books
Plymouth, Wisconsin

Against the Odds: Six Projects and Letters to the Six Intrepid Colleagues-in-Arms Who Helped to Change Small Pieces of the World
by Belden Paulson
© 2018 Thistlefield Books

ISBN: 978-0-9816906-6-7
Library of Congress Control Number: 2018944749

Cover photo: Loch Ness in Scotland, the magical land where a vision for a new kind of global future lighted fires under so many.
Back cover Photo of Bel and Lisa Paulson by Robert M. Overdahl, courtesy of *The Milwaukee Journal Sentinel*

Design and Production: Kate Hawley by Design
Proofreader: Paula Haubrich

Thistlefield Books

W7122 County Road U
Plymouth, Wisconsin 53073
(920)528-8488 • www.ThistlefieldBooks.com

For Lisa

This small book is dedicated to you, the love of my life.

As college classmates who never met until several years after graduation

in war-ruined Naples, Italy, we've continued to share

more than 60 years of adventures. You've participated in and

contributed mightily to all the experiences recounted here,

and also worked closely with me to polish and enrich the letters.

Table of Contents

Introduction

Ten years ago I sat down to write what I thought would be a letter about my life to my four grandchildren. As the memories piled up, I found myself writing more and more, and eventually ended up with over a thousand pages.

I managed to reduce this unwieldy tome somewhat, and after some urging from friends and colleagues, the "letter" became my book, *Odyssey of a Practical Visionary*.

Two years ago our first great grandchild, Leonardo, joined the family. Shortly thereafter, once again I decided to sit down to write another letter. Since I expected to have left the planet by the time he was fully able to comprehend my epistle, I tried to be brief. I wanted to make sure Leo would actually read it. Disciplining myself to stop at 50 pages, my product was *Conversation with Leo: Highlights from the Life Journey of his Great-Grandfather*.

Now, while I was reflecting on significant and unforgettable past adventures, some inner voice once again has pushed me into more letter writing. This time I've picked out six distinct episodes in my long journey and identified one key colleague in each with whom to reminisce about the exciting work we created together. Each letter or project might in itself merit a small book, but I've brought them together here in deliberately abbreviated synopses. My readers will thank me for keeping each letter to only slightly more than 20 pages!

Belden Paulson

Rescuing refugees as meaningful for Don Murray as an acting career

Dear Don,

Where to begin? It could be when we first met in Naples in 1953. We were both in our twenties, both volunteers working in the bombed-out ruins of one of Europe's worst postwar slums.

Maybe I should start with when you visited Lisa and me one night at our "hut" on the Midway at the University of Chicago. You'd just finished the film *Bus Stop* with Marilyn Monroe, and we talked about a new collaboration.

Or when we recognized that our refugee project in Sardinia might not make it, notwithstanding all the blood and treasure we had invested—now perhaps admitting defeat just as the world authorities had told us would happen.

Or when we'd completed the first lap of our pioneering effort in 1959, when the project had begun to demonstrate success in realizing our early intentions, and now the positive results were being circulated widely.

This letter to you details several of the most formative years in my earlier life, and it's my guess that our time together in Italy was the same for you.

For both of us we might say this was a time of more or less pure idealism. We weren't out to make money. Exercising power was the last thing on our minds. Our goal was to use our talents and resources, modest as they were, to contribute in some small way to solving a major world problem. We were just starting out with a head of steam and not too much else. Presumably you had already begun to envisage an acting career, with expectation of a rosy future. I was finishing a rigorous graduate study program, with the likely goal of moving into government or academia.

We've talked about this, and while you may not admit it, I surmised that your full commitment to our project had some impact on your career as an actor. It also affected your marriage. I remember when I stayed at your house; it was almost bare of furniture because your resources were going into our project. In my own case, I set aside years of academic preparation for an unknown future as we embarked on our project, and along the way I almost lost my wife due to a health crisis.

When we began we had little sense as to how to proceed. Respected authorities warned us that although they admired our motivation and enthusiasm, the complex problems we faced were miles above our heads. In essence, they said we were wasting our own time and the resources of others.

I'm writing you now in the Age of Trump. In succeeding Barack Obama as U.S. president, he represents a completely different world of experience; some say he is clearly unfit to be president. A billionaire with very limited exposure to the workings of government, he has appointed tycoons and generals to key positions. We might need a microscope to explore every crevice of his life and in the government he is forming to find the kind of idealism I'm writing about in this letter. He has surprised everyone thus far; who knows, his footprint is unpredictable as to the future.

You and I arrived in Europe only a few years after World War II. The continent was shattered, millions were dead, and there was devastating hunger everywhere. But then there were great moments: outstanding world leaders emerged to rebuild the infrastructure and restore the confidence of new generations. We now know that the institutions formed in that period, which have served well for 70 years, are under pressure as never before. This was confirmed in our elections of 2016. People are restless and angry and are demanding change, but with little sense as to what they are invoking.

This letter in no way analyzes those changes or proposes models for today's critical problems. My goal is to capture the motivation that spurred us then and our creative efforts to translate our idealism into practical results. Let us imagine—or hope—that these same kinds of values might infiltrate the ranks of today's youth and leaders.

Don, I wish you were sitting next to me and that our conversation was face to face! But since a couple of thousand miles separate your California from my Wisconsin, I'll quickly refresh your memory with some lines about my life leading up to our meeting and collaboration.

When I finished college in the early 1950s, I had a strong desire to get involved in Europe's reconstruction, but I had few contacts and little money. Luckily, Joe Howell of the national

Congregational Church and World Council of Churches steered my thinking. He advised me to join the international Agape work camp in the Italian Alps. Joe arranged for me to take a student ship from Quebec to Le Havre.

A hundred young people from 22 countries were building a spectacular center for conferences. For a month I carried rocks up the steep mountainside that the masons used for construction. Joe had suggested to Teofilo Santi, a dedicated medical doctor from Naples, that the doctor stop to interview me at the work camp while on his honeymoon. He was looking for volunteers to assist him in his humanitarian work with the homeless still living in caves after the war. We hit it off and he promised to cover my subsistence if I'd commit to work with him for at least six months.

I should add that I had enlisted three college classmates to join me for the European adventure: the student ship, biking for a month across the Swiss Alps, and then showing up at the work camp. Three of us also went on to work together for some months in Naples, but I ended up staying for almost three years.

You, too, Don, remember the Naples of that period. The surrounding scenery was incredible—the mesmerizing Mediterranean Sea and mile-high volcano, Mt. Vesuvius—but the city itself was in wretched shape. Homes had been decimated from years of bombing, first by the Allies and then the Germans. Packs of children roamed like animals, chasing up cigarette butts that they "manufactured" into cigarettes to sell. Unemployment was catastrophic and government policy to improve conditions almost non-existent. Santi urged us to "go slow, don't let yourselves get overwhelmed, take on one problem at a time."

One of our creative efforts was to visit ships from the American Sixth Fleet based in the harbor, and collect quantities of surplus food for the starving. One day, we brought large boxes of meat and bread to distribute among the 28 families in Capodimonte Cave. The food was supposed to be for the children, but a hungry man lunged for it. A pregnant woman screamed curses at him and he kicked her in the stomach. She fell unconscious. A fight broke out and general chaos ensued. My American colleague and I grabbed the food that was left and got out fast.

With Santi and our small staff, we talked about the fight and agreed that, important as it was to keep people alive, we needed to find longer-term solutions. The doctor closed his medical clinic in the cave, and temporarily we withheld all aid.

Since I knew about social settlement centers from my parents—years ago, my mother had worked with Jane Addams at Hull House in Chicago—I urged that we consider such a strategy here. The basic idea was to organize a center right in the middle of the worst neighborhood. By concentrating in one place all of our resources—medical clinic, educational programs ranging from kindergarten to adult classes, handcraft training, and athletics, plus direct material assistance—we could make a real impact. We focused on entire families. Our model and influence, in turn, could stimulate others. We found a building to rent, remodeled it, and named it "Casa Mia" (My Home). We were told this was the first social settlement center in Italy.

Even though this waterfront slum was considered lawless and dangerous, we became a familiar presence. Our center evolved into an oasis for the homeless, a "second home." Although our project was small, and because the city powers had far less knowledge of the needs than our staff, we were noticed and our influence spread.

After a number of months, a couple of young American women showed up late one night at Casa Mia. After a long day, I was ready for bed when suddenly I heard a loud banging on the center's big iron gate. I thought there might be some emergency, but was amazed to see these two exhausted visitors shouldering knapsacks. Although they had had no address, a bunch of street kids who knew us led them to the center. Lisa Hill was actually a classmate of mine from Oberlin College, although we'd never met. I fed them and arranged for Dr. Santi to put them up for the night at his orphanage in the suburbs. The next morning he called me, mentioning that one of them would return to Rome for a job at the U.N. What to do with Lisa Hill? On the strength of the fact she was from Oberlin, and we certainly needed help, I suggested we hire her as a volunteer. (By that time, my bicycling friends had moved on.) Lisa quickly learned the language and the work, and a year later we left Naples together. Six months later, we were married.

You, Don, were the second important person to enter my life in Naples in this period. Two days before Lisa and I departed for America, you arrived, appointed as my successor to direct Casa Mia. As a C.O. (conscientious objector), you had begun working as a volunteer in Germany with the Church of the Brethren. Then you were drawn to accept this special assignment in Naples. Over two days, we gave you a whirlwind orientation tour. You met many folks, visited a refugee camp 30 miles outside the city where we provided assistance, and we discussed strategy with Dr. Santi.

I assumed you'd have the same kind of fantastic experience I had. You'd learn, in-depth, about the aftermath of war, not abstractly, but by being in touch every day with the human beings who had paid the terrible price. Even though you might not solve the big problems, you'd be amazed, as I was, at the rippling effects of the caring and love you could bring. For example, I will never forget the tragic day when a 14-year-old girl who had enthusiastically attended Casa Mia, suddenly died of a kidney disease. Lisa and I showed up at their hovel for the wake where sobbing throngs of homeless people were gathered. We were especially moved by what happened the next day. According to custom, the horse-drawn funeral procession, before proceeding to the cemetery, solemnly passed by the place the deceased had most cherished. The cortege came to our Casa Mia gate, where it stopped for a moment of silence.

I didn't hear from you for almost a year. Then came a four-page report, with excerpts here:

> I expected when I came here to accept the responsibility and authority that you had, Bel. It was because of the importance of this work and the inspiration of what I saw here on my visit, which caused me to leave the Brethren and my German friends. . . . I thought this was the "breaking in" period in which I would be able to just feel my way

around and learn the language before being worked into my responsibilities as director of the center. Unfortunately, I became ill soon after my arrival (stomach trouble), and have never been really well since. . . . I was urged, practically ordered, to take it easy. Now, after two months away from work with yellow jaundice, the picture of how this absence is handily being used to help preserve the status quo is even more evident. . . . This is the most difficult, exasperating eight months I ever hope to see.

You went on to list a number of successful activities you had organized, but you never worked into my responsibilities. You recognized that I had developed a trusting relationship with Santi, which allowed me to introduce democratic procedures with our staff. While he admired my approach, now that I was gone he reverted to his top-down, autocratic ways. You wrote that Santi's "energy and devotion are all but overwhelming. I really love the guy, but I find him all but impossible to work with." You noted the impact I'd made on the staff, as well as on Santi, and that someday you'd like to work directly with me again. You concluded: "I promised when you left that I'd take care of your baby, but the tyke got kidnapped before I ever got there. Although she's healthy, I don't think she's growing in the way she should."

You urged me to write Dr. Ballou. He was director of the Congregational Church agency that provided major support for the Naples operation. You wanted me to emphasize that an American should be director of Casa Mia, even though it might not be you. Since Ballou was very close to and respectful of Dr. Santi, I'm sure that anything critical I said about Santi would create quite a stir. I did write Ballou a six-pager, and we had some significant correspondence about the future of the Naples work.

Once accepting your changed role, you found a great outlet for your talents. This was the refugee problem. There were five camps outside of Naples teeming with hundreds of refugees who were either displaced persons from the war or escapees from communism in Eastern Europe. Thousands had passed through camps in Europe to new homes, but what was left now were the so-called "hard-core." They'd been rejected for emigration to other countries because of health problems or a host of other handicaps. Few solutions had been found to integrate them into the surrounding society. Santi had arranged that, along with the Casa Mia project, we would link with the World Council of Churches to offer social assistance to refugees in these barbed-wire camps.

You described the refugees' "hopeless imprisonment of guiltless people," and that this meager aid given them was like "visiting a condemned man with candy." You spent a lot of time with them, wrote stories about them, and were full of ideas to produce a movie about the refugee problem. You said you'd found another "mission in life—refugees." Santi was supportive of your efforts in this changed role and continued providing your subsistence stipend.

You and I had no contact again for two years. In September 1956, I read something in the *New York Times* that said you had just finished the film *Bus Stop* with Marilyn Monroe.

You were being heralded as a fresh new face in Hollywood, but you also stressed your continuing strong interest in refugees. I wrote a note of congratulation, and in particular asked what you had in mind regarding the refugee situation. You responded that you had to do something about the refugees you personally had gotten to know in Naples, and you wanted very much to see me.

You wrote again from Hollywood that you'd be in Chicago at the end of October, and that we had to meet. Little could either of us envisage what was in store for us!

Before I get into the project that consumed us for the next years, and which will take the rest of this letter, I want to share several reflections about my time in Naples. My guess is that you had similar thoughts.

First, a word about communism. Today, this subject has been replaced by our concerns about Islam and other international issues, but when we were in Naples in the early 1950s, the Cold War was close to becoming hot. While the U.S. was disarming after having built up its huge wartime military, the USSR was becoming more and more aggressive. There was even talk that it might move into Western Europe. Italy had become a key player. Since the Italian Communist Party, with its indigenous partisan leadership, had helped the Allies end Mussolini's reign and win back the country, the Party was now close to taking over the government through free elections—the first such event in the West. Most of the people who came to Casa Mia said they voted communist, although they had little idea about politics. I talked to many of them and knew them well; they were genuine idealists simply demanding radical change. The American authorities urged us at Casa Mia to use our influence, but we refused; our work was non-political and our motivation was service. I met ex-communist leaders who had left the Party once they realized that the Party's pseudo-idealism was mainly to win power.

I observed all the ineffective local anti-communist activity going on in Italy, and then later when I returned home I was appalled at the strident anti-communist propaganda sweeping America. I remembered the amazing impact of our influence at Casa Mia because our power was based on compassion. It was incredible how the community had turned to us. In the next years I ran into many other Casa Mia-type initiatives and saw the huge influence they generated. I consulted with officials in our foreign aid program and wrote widely on the positive alternatives we'd experimented with as a strategy to improve life conditions and, along the way, to effectively confront communism.

Second, I learned something about social change. In Naples, as in so much of war-destroyed Europe then, the problems seemed overwhelming. While we dealt with the economic and political and social issues, often there was a missing element. This had to do with the underlying culture—the values. My mother, who had worked in similar conditions in war-torn Poland just after WW I, wrote me a couple of letters each week. Although she was now a semi-invalid, she had developed profound insights after a prominent social work career. I paraphrase one letter:

> I've been thinking a lot lately about your project. Its success both in the accomplishments in material ways and in its inspirational value with others, has to do with spirit. Some of the "greats" I worked with were far above other social workers in my day in formulating methods that brought change, because they had a willingness to acknowledge the spiritual aspect of working in depth. Other workers created great new methods that helped the public welfare ... but they missed out on the element of spirit. I believe the creative dare, the unexplainable insights that well up from the depths of one's spirit, the faith that cannot be reasoned through, the belief in potentialities in human beings beyond all proof of reason, the desire to serve—all these belong in this category of spirit. They ultimately bring change at the deepest level. As the most challenging problems come to light, they have to be attacked not only with reason and clear proof of success, but with this inner faith to trust in your own creative instincts as to how to proceed. Your project is not a religious enterprise. It is an enterprise of spirit.

Third, there was dealing with other cultures. When I arrived in Europe the first time, I suddenly realized that I belonged to a very small minority group. People looked pretty much the same, but they spoke a different language. When we biked across the Alps we had to figure out how to negotiate with Swiss farmers to sleep in their barns. At the international work camp there were many languages, but we quickly learned how to carry rocks up the mountain together. I was moved when I was part of a small work party where there was a young American and also a young German; both had fought in the Battle of the Bulge, trying to kill each other. While now they had trouble with their languages, they found a way to communicate. After I arrived in Naples and we organized Casa Mia in the middle of the slum, two of us lived at the center. Antonio, an Italian about my age, and I were roommates. While we had a small staff under the overall direction of Dr. Santi, who showed up periodically, the two of us ran the center. I had to learn Italian and he picked up some English. I had finished college while he had barely gotten through high school. Our background worlds were very different yet we became very close, assisting each other over long hours of stress and toil carrying out multiple activities with hundreds of hungry, homeless people. We confronted every possible kind of conflict. When I left Naples Antonio said: "You are not just my friend, you are my brother in the true sense of the word. You and I found the force to overcome every obstacle."

Don, you developed your own close relationships in Naples, especially with the refugees in the camps. After years, they had lost all hope to live. You learned to understand them. Our time in Naples may have been a starting point for each of us. We learned to pack away some of our own culture and open up to that of others. We learned about radically different lifestyles and habits. At the beginning I was very judgmental—how could I get along with the autocratic Dr.

Santi? Later on, he and I matured into a special relationship. I doubt that you and I could have survived our later project together without this Naples test. Much later in life, when I worked in other cultures such as in Brazil and China, and also found deep-level kindred relationships in our African-American inner city communities, I always looked back to Naples.

Lisa and I had been on the University of Chicago campus for two and half years. I'd finished my master's degree and all my courses and exams for the Ph.D. But the big hurdle remained: writing the dissertation. Our son, Eric, had just been born, and we were getting ready to leave our prefab hut on campus to stay with my folks for several weeks in Oak Park, a Chicago suburb. Then Lisa and Eric would move to Schenectady, N.Y. to live with her parents while I finished up in Oak Park. Hopefully, by summer I'd graduate, find a job, and then we'd set up a household together—settling, really, for the first time since we married in 1954.

You, Don, had returned from Naples, and in fall 1956 you'd just filmed *Bus Stop* and were about to shoot your second film, *Bachelor Party*. You and Hope Lange, your actress wife, were getting rave reviews. When interviewers asked you what it was like to kiss Marilyn Monroe, you changed the subject to your strongest priority, the desperate refugee problem. After I wrote you to applaud your continued refugee commitment, you mentioned that you'd be in Chicago at the end of October. You wrote, "It's important that we meet."

You arrived by cab at 10 p.m. and the three of us reminisced about Italy most of the night. Despite your new fame you had no swelled head. We talked about the dire challenges we'd faced in Naples. You were emphatic about the necessity of going back to Europe to get some of those refugees out of the barbed-wire camps. You pushed hard for my help. I said that much as I'd like to help, my involvement would be very difficult at this moment. Further, I knew of no strategy to clear the refugee camps, although I agreed this was a great humanitarian problem.

On second thought, I did mention one idea. While I was in Naples, the World Council of Churches commissioned a small group of us to visit Falerna, a town in Calabria, one of Italy's poorest regions. Falerna had let it be known it would accept a few refugees if our group would buy land and create some agricultural jobs and small industries. This clearly would help to revitalize the local community. If successful, our pilot effort would be a model for others. While the idea didn't go anywhere, you liked this vision. You suggested now that the two of us return to Italy to take a look at Falerna and other locations. I agreed to at least help conceptualize a project.

Ten days after Lisa, Eric and I moved to Oak Park, you called from New York, asking me to meet you there. You and Hope were leaving shortly for Italy to publicize your films. This would be a great opportunity for you to contact the refugee authorities, including the United Nations. You'd ask if they would support an eventual project sponsored by you. While I had some important university meetings that I'd miss, Lisa said, "GO, just do it." (How many times was I to hear those words!) We spent a whole day together at your New York hotel. I agreed that if the authorities you met on your trip were really supportive, I'd agree to return to Italy with you to study the possibility that this could contribute to solving the refugee problem.

On New Years Eve you called again from New York to report on the European trip. We talked for an hour. You had met United Nations refugee officials in Geneva and the Italian Ministry of Interior; everyone was positive. You saw Dr. Santi in Naples; he was enthusiastic seeing you and threw a party. Now you wanted me to come to New York in late January to develop more details for a possible project.

Since by now the word had gotten out about this "far-out intention" to help solve the refugee problem, both my family and Lisa's were pressing me NOT to go any further. They told me Don was a special friend and an impressive actor, and refugees were a serious world problem. But I had to put first things first: finish the Ph.D. in which I'd invested a lot, secure a regular job and take care of my wife and baby. It was a nice way of implying that it was time to quit sponging off our two families. This was not the time for another exotic adventure!

Since Lisa and little Eric were in Schenectady staying with her folks while I was in Oak Park writing my thesis, I rationalized that meeting you in New York would give me time to work on the thesis in Schenectady while also being with my family. I could also use the New York libraries. You called several more times, really pumped up.

I found you on the 26th floor of the St. Moritz hotel overlooking Central Park. You were busy shooting *A Hatful of Rain*, but were eager to talk. We kept going non-stop from 2:00 p.m. to 8:30 p.m., ordering in dinner. Were a project to emerge, you and Hope would serve as project cochairs. If I were to commit for one year, I'd be project director. Brethren Service and the Congregational Church overseas committee would help with administration. In the spring we'd take an exploratory trip to Italy. While in New York I met a bunch of agencies I knew from Naples days that could be helpful. They were all enthusiastic about the project. Lisa came into the city for us to join you and Hope for a private showing of your new film, *Bachelor Party*.

Once back home, I didn't hear from you for several weeks, which was fine because I could concentrate on my writing. I did take a little time to outline my thinking, were a project ever to materialize. We had discussed the 40,000 refugees still in Europe, including the thousands in Italy who had been stranded in camps for years with no solution. With emigration largely closed off because of the refugees' multiple handicaps, authorities were looking for ways to integrate them into the local economies where the camps were located. But this had proven almost impossible because of the huge national unemployment. The authorities had also concluded that after years in camps, these refugees were unlikely to ever become self-sufficient. However, our project would challenge this assumption because we knew the refugees personally. With our help, at least some of them could become independent.

An essential part of our strategy to win support of the Italian government, and also the community where we'd base the project, would be to boost local economic development. Thus, as a starting point, why not take another look at struggling Falerna?

In conclusion, I wrote you: "This is a big order but we know that most projects begin with a good idea as well as big obstacles. People say 'it can't work' and often it doesn't work.

That's why individuals and small dedicated groups like us are out front. We're unlikely to see our government or the Italian government experimenting with questionable solutions. We are the pioneers and we'll approach this with the attitude that we will succeed."

You replied that you liked what I wrote. You were very aware that our project was experimental: "It may work out beautifully and it may be a dismal failure. But it is worth trying if we're sure of two factors: the strong enthusiasm of the refugees who would take part, and a really positive participation by the Italian governmental authorities. If these factors can't be assured absolutely and definitely, I believe the risk of time and money would be too great." As an alternative, which would be doing at least something, you said you'd arrange to send two Brethren Service volunteers to work in the camps. I said that in that case, I'd no longer be involved. But we both agreed that a survey was the first essential step.

On April 7 you called from Hollywood and said *Bachelor Party* would be featured at the Cannes Film Festival in France in early May. You were entitled to a first class ticket but would exchange it for two tourist tickets for both of us. We needed to set a date to meet in Rome.

My mind was getting cluttered with mixed messages. I badly wanted to meet you in Rome, but I knew that if the best happened and a project proved feasible, the pressure would be overwhelming for me to drop everything else and commit to do it. Should I meet now with Professor Finer, my primary adviser on my doctoral committee at the University of Chicago, to show him what I'd written? He had already approved my initial outline. Or should I wait until I finished the first draft, after returning from Italy?

Various people were asking me to consider attractive jobs that would eliminate the mounting family pressure I was feeling: to prioritize taking care of my family (instead of a very risky uncertain refugee project, not to mention working mostly as a volunteer). An eminent United Nations consultant recently back from overseas development assignments said I was a prime candidate for a U.N. appointment. My favorite relative, Uncle Ben, said he was nearing retirement and urged me to consider joining his lucrative advertising business; he'd like to keep the business in the family. Lisa wrote me with her usual supportive wisdom: "What an unusual and marvelous husband I have . . . putting things in the exacting perspective of your value system. . . . It makes me so happy and excited to think I will be a 'pioneer' again. I doubt whether we'll ever fall into the pit of stagnation that so many have. . . ."

I gave my partly finished thesis to Professor Finer and promised to see him as soon as I returned from Italy.

Rome was beautiful as we flew in on April 16. It was almost four years since I'd left Italy, but it seemed like yesterday. You were arriving from Geneva after meeting United Nations and World Council of Churches officials. I'd meet you at your hotel. You called Dr. Livio Malfetanni, head of the Italian Cooperative movement—he knew everyone. He called a key politician in South Italy who arranged our visit to Falerna. The next day we were in the refugee camps to renew contact with three refugees you had been close to when in Naples: Roubal and Nyc, two Czechs, and deAngelini, a Yugoslav. They'd all been in the camps for years and would be our first project participants.

The next three days we were in Calabria meeting top officials. The local communist government in Falerna and the mayors and town notables in other villages promised us all kinds of concessions. Of course they assumed we were rich Americans and we'd bring with us the American movie industry. We returned to Rome and met Dr. Schlatter, head of the UNHCR Italy office, and others. He said every effort to integrate refugees into the Italian economy had failed thus far. Italian officials were very skeptical about taking into the economy anti-communist foreign refugees from Eastern Europe when the communist Left was threatening to win national elections.

Despite all the promises of support in Calabria and official interest in Rome, nothing clicked for us. You remember how we were at a loss as to our next move. What now? Since you had to leave to fly to Cannes, a young Brethren volunteer serving in Germany, Ken Kreider, joined me. The next day Dr. Malfetanni took Ken and me to meet the head of *La Cassa per il Mezzogiorno*, the billion dollar Italian agency to develop South Italy. I described what happened in a letter home:

> We were lifted out of our chairs when the director, Engineer Orcel, told us that if we wanted favorable conditions, the ideal spot with everything in our favor was Sardinia. He said, "The island is just now opening up, land is relatively cheap but fertile, natural resources abound, it's spectacularly beautiful for tourism, with pristine beaches, mountains and wild game." *La Cassa* would help us financially and provide experts. Sardinia had been a penal colony in the past, devastated by malaria until after the war when the Rockefeller Foundation spent $15 million to spray the entire island with DDT.

Malfetanni encouraged us to travel to Sardinia immediately. Ken and I returned to the hotel, planning to take the train to Naples and the ship to Cagliari, the island's capital. Who should walk in at that moment but you—your plane had motor trouble so you were delayed. You were thrilled with the Sardinia idea and only regretted that you couldn't join us.

The next three weeks until my return to America was one of the most scintillating and exhausting periods of my life. The director of ETFAS, Sardinia's large-scale land reform agency, agreed to lend us one of his chief assistants, Emma Morin. She knew Sardinia intimately, and in the past had worked in the refugee camps.

We drove north along the western coast, stopping along the way to get a feel for the island. An hour north, we ended up in Oristano, a bustling town near the coast. She introduced us to Dr. Bruno Sanna, who ran the agricultural and technical operations of the *Consorzio di Bonifica*. This was the semi-governmental agency committed to economic development of the entire region. He was a visionary and immediately saw the potential of our project. We'd transform virgin land into irrigated, productive agriculture, create small businesses, and build refugee homes. We'd add value to the local economy. We could receive a 38 percent subsidy from the national government and 12 percent from the region for most of our development costs.

We also met Professor Giovanni Pau. He taught law, but his real interest was serving as president of the *Consorzio*, and managing lands he owned. After checking various properties, we kept returning to the 135-acre tract he owned, located not far from Oristano. Nearby we visited Simaxis, the village where our refugee families could mingle with the local people. Both Pau and Sanna promised maximum help because our successful project would benefit the region.

Ken Kreider had to return to Germany temporarily, but Emma Morin and I explored the area in greater depth. We met the communist mayor and Catholic priest of Simaxis. Both welcomed us with open arms. The more we examined all the ramifications of a project, the more doable it appeared.

Back in Rome I reported on our efforts to all the relevant actors. They seemed not only interested but enthusiastic. I returned to the camps and spent more time with the refugees, and especially your old friends from Naples days. They promised they'd welcome being the first recruits in our project. I invested a lot of time with Elena Buonocuore, the UNHCR representative in the camps. She was the smartest, most experienced contact for refugee work in Italy. After all her years dealing with the idle, dependent refugees, she was wary of all so-called solutions. Nevertheless, she gave our project a fighting chance because we—especially you, Don—knew some of the refugees personally.

I felt the next step before communicating with you again was to discuss the whole endeavor with M.R. Ziegler in Geneva. He headed all the Brethren work in Europe, was a man of vast experience and a hardheaded idealist. I took a train to Geneva, and after hearing all the details, he agreed that we should call you. Since this effort was turning into a much bigger, more expensive and complex initiative than we'd ever talked about, I didn't know what you'd think. Everyone agreed that if we could pull it off, it promised a great impact. Admittedly, this was a very formidable IF. Before the call, I met with leaders in the UNHCR offices at their Geneva headquarters. I was surprised to learn that this sort of project had never actually been tried. No one had thought of combining refugee resettlement with economic development as a viable strategy. They recognized that this model could offer wide application for the broad refugee problem, far beyond our project.

I called you in California and explained all the details. The land purchase would be $50,000. The entire project tab was unknown, but the initial cost would come to more than $100,000. Perhaps we could find half from Italian and U.N. agencies. Could you find the other half? There was silence and I sensed a couple of gulps. Then you said: "LET'S DO IT! But don't make any commitments yet, like buying land." M.R. said he knew you'd say Yes.

Before leaving Italy I spent more time in the camps with Buonocuore and the refugees, and with the agencies in Rome. Ken and I took a final quick trip back to Sardinia, getting permission from a camp director to take Roubal and Nyc, your two favorite refugees, with us. We arranged with the camp authorities and the United Nations to consider allowing three refugees to spend the summer on the land in Sardinia with Ken. This would be a test to see what would happen. Pau agreed that we could use his land, with the expectation we'd soon buy it.

As I flew home, a cluster of scenarios flooded my head. This project had suddenly gotten big with its interdependent moving parts—the refugees, officials and authorities from multiple entities, and our plan to actually organize businesses. Could it all work? Could you find the money? Would the various agencies fulfill their promises? And the great unknown: could we prove the authorities wrong, demonstrating that at least some refugees after years in camps, could still become self-sufficient?

But on other subjects: What if Professor Finer rejected my thesis draft and I couldn't return soon to Sardinia to run the project? While I thought that Lisa and Hope would swallow hard but support us, what about our parents? I knew my folks and also Lisa's believed that this new foreign adventure was not only unwise but could be a wild goose chase. Could a couple of young guys like us, admitted idealists, pull off such an enterprise?

Most importantly, on one point I felt that you and I were agreed: if we gave it our all, the essence of the project was valid and doable. I predicted that:

+ We'd get some refugees out of the camps, and whatever it took, they'd make it;
+ We'd get support, both political and financial, from the UNHCR;
+ We'd get subsidies and expertise from the Italian development agencies;
+ We'd get the local community to accept them as new citizens;
+ We'd demonstrate to the authorities that our pilot effort could contribute to solving the larger problem.

Back home, in early June I met with you in New York. You had already written me: "Everything sounds very good and encouraging. I just have a few questions." In particular, were we getting a fair price for the land? If we're really going to help solve the refugee problem and we're able to settle the first ten families, how much bigger would the investment need to be to resettle many more people, in order to hold up our project as a feasible example? Can we rent with option to buy, so that if conditions change we're not stuck with a large land expense? All good questions.

It didn't take long to decide that we wanted to do the project. We'd negotiate for the best land price. Our goal was limited: to show that if some refugees could make it, then other entities with larger resources could move forward with our ideas and experience. We'd hold off Pau as long as possible before making a big land payment.

We had to get Ken Kreider and several refugees on the land for an initial test to see if the refugees were really up to working for a new life. We had to organize publicity to build support. I had to find a way to clear my deck at the university for a year or two. You had to find money for the start-up.

Lisa came down to New York from Schenectady to be with us. Here's what she wrote to her best friend:

> We had a marvelous time with Don and Hope and their new baby while planning and reviewing the findings of Bel's recent trip. Don had both his agent and one of the publicity heads of 20th Century Fox working on ways to raise money. They were full of enthusiastic ideas, one of which would put Don on every possible radio or TV show to tell the story. Hope was starting to work on *Peyton Place*. . . . Several reporters came in for interviews with the usual questions about how it feels to kiss Marilyn Monroe, but in no time Don was off on his whole philosophy and the project. He had them amazed and fascinated for more than an hour.

As I look back, this was one of our first high points; we had in our hands a significant initiative to help the world. We were four committed kindred spirits. While in New York, you and I appeared before the board of the national Congregational Church Service Committee for overseas work, the same body that earlier had supported our work in Naples with Dr. Santi. We would ask for money ($5,000) to cover my family's subsistence in Sardinia for one year, so that we would not have to use project dollars for this. Dr. Ballou, C.C.S.C. director, then wrote us: "If you fellows had asked us for the moon when you made your presentation, I think the committee was so excited they would have voted to give it to you. They were delighted that we're to have a part in this effort."

I returned with Lisa to her parents' home in Schenectady before heading west to Oak Park to finish work on the thesis. Of course, a main reason for me was also to see Eric, our 8-month-old son, who had been there all the time I was in Oak Park. Lisa's parents were extremely generous to host her and Eric, but in a friendly way they bombarded me with the same questions my own parents had asked. Isn't your first priority to finish the Ph.D., then worry about refugees? What kind of job will this project prepare you for when you return? When you're young and free as you were in Naples with no wife and child, you could gamble. No one now wanted to discuss money and my committing to work almost as a volunteer. Don, I wonder if anyone was asking you similar relevant questions about your life. How would this project's big commitment affect your acting career and your family?

Back in Oak Park, my first assignment was to visit Professor Finer to get his assessment of my first draft of the thesis. While in Italy I had rarely thought about the Ph.D.

Finer had a cozy apartment near the university campus; he was an eminent professor and prolific author. He lauded my interest in the refugee problem. Then he dropped the bombshell. My thesis was unacceptable. He complimented me on my research; my material was innovative but was not political science. He said International Relations does not deal with individuals—it involves states and governments, political processes to resolve conflict, issues of war and peace. My master's thesis, "The Role of the Voluntary Agency in International Relations" had been so well received that I had been urged to expand it for the doctorate. Now I had to demonstrate how the humanitarian activities of non-governmental organizations influenced power relationships. He said all the good work and documentation I'd done need not be lost, but I had to revamp my conceptual model.

As I left, I was really disheartened. The more I analyzed my data, I had to conclude that this would be a time-consuming undertaking and might never pass muster.

Sardinia project pressures were mounting. Ken Kreider agreed to go to Sardinia for a month with three refugees (Roubal, Nyc, and a Spaniard, Tony). The director of ETFAS in Sardinia agreed to provide equipment and experts to begin to improve the land. Professor Pau said we could use his land for the trial period, but a down payment of $10,000 for the land was due as soon as I returned. The Brethren Service Committee had recruited an excellent young farmer, Harold Armstrong, who would commit to two years in Sardinia as a semi-volunteer. You called me regularly, and I said the earliest I could get to Sardinia would be the end of September. We agreed to meet in New York the third week in July for fund-raising.

Our first days in New York were depressing. The Rockefeller brothers turned us down, as did a number of others. Then we met Spiros Skouras in his luxurious office. He was president of your studio, 20th Century Fox. He was one of the world's richest men, also close to the Eisenhower administration. He was noncommittal, but asked us to contact his confidant, Amelia Girden. She was enthusiastic and helped us draft a letter that Skouras would sign and send to leaders in the motion picture business and companies for in-kind donations.

She also asked us to communicate with Dr. Kevin McCann, president of Defiance College and an Eisenhower speechwriter. McCann said our effort was exactly what Ike liked: young Americans courageously going out to solve problems beyond the capacity of government bureaucrats. Ike was playing golf in Rhode Island but we had 15 minutes with Vice President Nixon in Washington. Our best contact was Senator Hubert Humphrey; he said our project was precisely what was needed. He criticized the many agencies unable to close the refugee camps. He said he'd read our project into the Congressional Record and wanted to follow our progress.

Back in New York, we met Skouras again. He signed the letters and gave us $1,000. Our new farm manager, Harold Armstrong, was with us, along with Emilia Girden. You could tell Harold was right off the farm—quiet, sun-tanned, spoke with a drawl, a good solid guy, sort of scared of people. You asked him if he had a sports jacket—he put on his lumber jacket. Amelia told us afterward: "This was about the best theater I've seen. There was movie star Don, who looks and speaks dramatically. There was Bel, the doctor who was supposed to know all the answers. And there was Harold, a farmer flying to Sardinia in a couple of hours, young, idealistic, the dedicated prototype of the volunteer. I think it had the desired effect."

You and I were so stimulated by these adventures that we could hardly sleep and talked most of the night. We produced a small hard-hitting brochure, "A Message from Don Murray about the Homeless European Land Program—helping people now living behind barbed wire to a new life." From now on we used the acronym HELP. You wrote: "I am so convinced we will succeed that my wife and I are putting a large part of everything we earn into this project."

The various PR folks in the entertainment world who were helping us were no longer describing a small pilot project for a few families. They expanded our goal, saying that our intent was to close all the refugee camps in Europe. We'd also provide a model for resettling Arab refugees in the Middle East (an idea I'd previously briefly discussed). Your first three films were getting tremendous coverage in the press and Hollywood gossip columns. Often you mentioned HELP and included my name as your collaborator. Hedda Hopper wrote: "HELP has become worldwide in scope." And (creatively) in *Coronet*: "Now Don and his wife, actress Hope Lange, tithe their salaries to maintain a camp for 1,500 refugees near Naples."

Since our project as yet owned no land and had not yet even begun, you remember I asked you if we could limit these monstrous claims—they could get us into a sea of trouble. We discussed this issue and consulted with others, then decided we had no choice. Your entertainment world was our best source; it could generate far more publicity than anyone else—which was essential for our fund-raising. Even if full of inaccuracies.

In early July, Ken Kreider returned to Sardinia with three refugees. His colorful reports were surprisingly positive. Everyone was working hard to clear cactus from the land and plant crops. Our farmer, Harold Armstrong, arrived at the beginning of August and shortly thereafter Ken left. Soon Harold wrote that Professor Pau was demanding the $10,000 down payment, and that this was becoming an intolerable situation. I wrote Pau with the excuse that we were still waiting for permits from the Italian Government to bring more refugees to Sardinia. Harold Row, head of the Brethren Service Commission handling our administrative home office affairs, spent three days in Sardinia. He was impressed with the project, but wrote me an urgent letter: "HELP is in an early delicate state. You are badly needed as soon as possible."

At the beginning of September, Roubal, the smartest and most articulate of the refugees, wrote me a 12-page letter. Dense with details about everything that had happened in their two months in Sardinia, he was positive about the project's "huge potential." But he admitted that the three refugees were beginning to wonder, Is this project for real? They had a lot of faith in you, Don, but would this turn out to be one more refugee failure? Would the money materialize? Would the Italian authorities ever give permits for more refugees to leave the camps? He said Harold was a good farmer, but didn't speak Italian and had a hard time relating to the three of them. Roubal was still enthusiastic, but to save the project, I had to arrive at once.

You contacted me saying that in one way or another you'd find $25,000 startup money. This was not the $100,000 we'd projected for the first year, including for the land payment, but it would get us going. Amelia Girden wrote us about how she admired our efforts but that the efforts of Skouras had not produced much.

I was working hard to prepare something for Finer, but deep down I knew I faced an intellectual bottleneck. My thesis required radical restructuring. It would take time and I had not communicated any of this to you, Don, or to my close families. I did have an excuse for some delay because my sister had just announced she was getting married at the beginning of September, and she needed me to be there.

Decision: I would leave for Sardinia with my family after the wedding. I'd urge Lisa to start preparing. We'd take a ship from New York. I'd tell both sets of parents that I felt I had no choice other than to direct the project. I wrote to Harold and the refugees and the various agencies. I told Pau that he'd soon get his first $10,000. I asked Roubal and Harold to find us a place to live in Oristano or Simaxis. You wrote me your delight: "The exciting moment has at last arrived. *Buon viaggio e tutti auguri di buon successo del nostro progetto!*" You added: "Eleven-month-old Eric will be the first red-headed Italian they've ever seen."

Today, 60 years later, as I look back, this HELP project was pure High Risk. Don Murray and Belden Paulson were setting out to work closely with and to rehabilitate refugees who had been stagnating for years in camps. Just about everyone had given up on them. We had personal experience that propelled and bolstered us, no matter what everyone else said. We had no clear idea what it would cost or how to start out. We were going to Sardinia—an inviting but unknown place—with a concept that was original but unproven: to resettle hard-core refugees while also lifting a local area economically.

We were two young men who could claim some background, but this was nothing compared to the professionals who had worked for years with these refugees. Our small staff consisted of young semi-volunteers, not the usual well-paid, middle-aged veterans. I was bringing my wife and small child to this island, postponing my doctorate. You and your wife, two promising actors in the early stages of your careers, were committing much of your creative energy, not to mention money, to this enterprise. Looking back now, knowing what we know, what do you think? Were we wise to go ahead? Taking everything into account, my answer is still Yes. What about you?

Our 10-day boat trip from New York to Naples was not an auspicious start. Before we reached the mid-Atlantic Lisa's slight cold had turned into bronchitis. By the end of the voyage the bronchitis had morphed into nasty boils that became progressively worse. By the time we reached Sardinia she could hardly sit down. Eric had developed severe diarrhea and vomiting that worsened. With Lisa's pain and Eric's pitiful crying, my brain was already registering the loud and clear comments from the folks back home: "We told you so. This whole venture is a disaster." On arrival, I quickly got status reports from Harold and the three refugees. They had been there for three months, first with Ken and then Harold. They were all living on the land in a run-down, three-bedroom shack. The freshly whitewashed building sparkled in the glow of the late afternoon sun. A little propane tank fed a lamp bulb. They had made screens for the windows and door (screens were unheard of on the island). Drinking water was still carried from the railroad substation a couple hundred yards away. They bathed in the Tirso River running past the land. Their food was from CARE packages, plus some early vegetable production and the local market.

ETFAS, the development and land reform agency, had provided heavy equipment to level three hectares of land for irrigation canals. The group had removed bushels of stones, cut out enormous cacti, and planted one hectare, mainly in artichokes and grain. I was impressed. Away from the dependent idle living in the camp, the refugees had worked hard and survived in primitive conditions. Now, the rainy season was beginning and Harold was feeling as discouraged as the refugees—the folks who had been living in camps since the end of WW II. The Italian authorities had only given them temporary permission to leave the camps. I later heard that the government was sure the project would fail.

My first letter to you read:

> The project gives one the feeling of overwhelming problems but also great hope. Our challenge is to face the problems one at a time so that no one gets too discouraged. This is really a frontier, with all the opportunities and difficulties of breaking new ground. The refugees themselves say that after all they've been through, the test is going to be whether they can make it through the first year.

Since the crew only had hand tools to work with, right away we returned to Cagliari to buy a tractor and agricultural equipment. We also ordered a machine that could make up to 3,000 concrete blocks per day. Professor Pau was delighted to receive his $10,000 down payment and promised full cooperation (of course expecting shortly all the money due to him). While I expected the best, I understood very well the risks confronting us. With these initial sizable outlays, and many more to come, would the refugees stick it out? Would the Ministry of Interior give permission for integration, and could we expect the local people to be willing partners?

Harold and I invested hours every day with Dr. Sanna and his staff at the *Consorzio di Bonifica* designing a development plan for the whole project. To receive funds from the government agencies we had to create a *Piano di Massimo della Trasformazione*. This was a plan that spelled out our overall vision for settling 15 families while contributing significantly to the local economy. Within this overarching goal, each specific sub-goal—leveling the land for irrigation, building the homes, creating small industries such as a poultry business, bringing electricity onto the property—required its own detailed plan, with both a technical design and budget. The overall plan and each component had to be approved. I made sure that at least one refugee accompanied us to each meeting; I wanted them to participate directly in the creative process of organizing their project.

In the nearby village of Simaxis I soon found we were dealing with *The Little World of Don Camillo*, the famous books about life in poor Italian villages. The priest had a virtual monopoly on not only the local spiritual life, but also the recreation. The communist mayor controlled the political world and issues of social justice. They worked together in somewhat friendly, somewhat comical, perpetual tension. Almost every night Harold and the refugees watched television in the priest's little theater. The mayor and his cohorts produced constant notices, often with loudspeakers and music, concerning the economy and public events. With Piero, the town's brightest young man, I set up a committee that included the priest, the mayor, and the local labor office to select workers for employment on the HELP land. Because the locals assumed that all Americans were either rich or movie actors, they expected we'd bring in drinking water and start great new industries. Simaxis received minimal aid from the national government because it was communist. We had to convince folks that ours was a shoestring operation, and that we were working mainly as volunteers so any funds we raised would directly benefit the refugees.

I began making regular runs to Rome, toiling from dawn to dusk, dealing with the many agencies and visiting the camps to select more refugees. I'd heard through the grapevine that there was waning interest in our project among some agencies, and also that our refugees were about ready to give up. I spent time in the camps with Elena Buonocuore, the true believer in the project. She invited refugees into her office to meet with me, keeping in mind our goal of 15 families. We drafted a letter for the camp directors, agreeing to offer three-month trial periods in Sardinia for prospective candidates. Every refugee had the same questions: "While the chance for a new life is intriguing, will I really ever receive the fruits of my labor? Will this new promise be empty like all the others?" I felt the trip went well and was in good spirits on returning to Oristano.

On opening the door, the roof fell in. Eric had been sick since the day I left with Asiatic flu, a high fever, continual vomiting and diarrhea. Lisa's boils had gotten so debilitating that she'd called in a local doctor. He gave her shots (I found out that these were with rusty needles wrapped in newspapers—with dire consequences several months later). I received word from Buonocuore that the refugees we'd picked decided they didn't want to come after all. She wrote: "The real reason is that they will actually have to work. Staying in camp is secure. There is nothing they have to think about. No decisions to make."

Our newest American volunteer, Giles Gamble, arrived. While Harold was an excellent farmer, he had trouble with the language and in winning refugee confidence. Giles had special gifts with both. Then a new refugee arrived—Mario. He was a Yugoslav who had been rejected by 14 commissions for emigration because he'd lost a lung to tuberculosis, so Sardinia was his last option. Before escaping into Italy, he'd been chased by both the Nazis and Tito communists. Like Roubal and Nyc, he'd become expert in playing the system in camp: manipulating whatever resources were available, organizing small businesses in gambling, prostitution and the like. I figured we'd try now to harness these same entrepreneurial skills.

After weeks of hard work with us, Dr. Sanna at the *Consorzio* became excited about our project. He convinced us that substantial funding would become available in due course, and that our development efforts would help the area significantly. The concrete block machine we had ordered arrived, and two refugees were trained to operate this business, using sand and gravel from the nearby Tirso river. ETFAS was employing three large bulldozers to prepare the remaining land for irrigation.

It was obvious that Lisa and I needed help to negotiate the local markets and handle the household chores (such as washing diapers in the bathtub). After searching in nearby villages on my Lambretta motor scooter, with Lisa and Eric hanging on for dear life (before we acquired a little Fiat), we found Angela. She was a beautiful young lady, semi-literate, who fit into our family perfectly and soon cultivated a loving relationship with Eric.

While these were positive signs, I was becoming more and more aware of the "refugee psychology." After years of living in one camp or another and receiving empty promises for new lives, they had mostly given up. They had no faith in anyone, yet this project offered one last strand of hope. They believed they were no good. "Just look at us," they said. They knew they had become a statistic that lived, and perhaps soon would die, in a refugee camp. With little chance to work in the local economy, they existed as wards of the camp administration.

I wrote to you:

We're dealing with people who have been broken, cast almost completely out of the orbit of life. It becomes a question of re-stimulating the human spirit, or what is left of it, of encouraging faith in the future, of drowning the bitterness and hatred of mankind that being a refugee engenders. For them this is a last chance.

In another letter:

We keep trying to convince them that this is their project. For now, we represent a kind of benevolent camp director. They are accommodating in making the "sacrifice" of leaving the camp's security to put in time here. Sometimes they make us feel they're doing us a favor in receiving the opportunities offered. My job of maintaining the morale of Harold and Giles (because they live with them 24 hours a day) is as important as anything I do with the refugees. The refugees complain of our incompetence, especially hitting on Harold who is working his heart out, although he's not a good communicator. Roubal withdraws and holds his gripes until a week or so after an event and then piles on the criticism. Mario, who admits his atheism and complete lack of faith in anything except animals, simply becomes apathetic. Tony blows his top openly, rough when it happens, but it passes like the torrid gusts of Sardinian wind.

This dark side of human nature is the experimental part of the project. When the refugees are working side by side, in the fleeting times when they feel they can move mountains, when a particular personal or collective joy seems to bury all these anxieties in a moment of optimism, then all of us feel it is worth the effort, that in a few years they will feel far removed from the memory of barbed-wire camps.

The money issue was now becoming acute. Before I had left for Sardinia we had agreed we'd start out with $25,000 working capital, plus $10,000 for the land down payment. But much of it had not arrived. You wrote me that you borrowed $10,000 from your agent, and that you and Hope had broken your own rule and hired a public relations firm to help find funds. You said you were constantly thinking about Sardinia while in the High Sierras shooting the film *From Hell to Texas*. I wondered how you could remember your lines and perform, while, at the same time, Sardinia was taking a heavy toll on your emotions.

Don, we had a tiger by the tail. Once the refugees were out of camp and with us, we were personally responsible for them until they actually became integrated. All in all, our own lives were on the line, seeking funds to stay in business, trying to figure out the refugee psychology. The agencies were cheering for us but they were wary, and they knew very well the pessimism of the Italian authorities.

Around Thanksgiving, when folks normally relax and prepare for the big feast, at this moment we had to make the fateful decision: are we ready to make a full commitment for the land without turning back? Pau was hounding us for the rest of his money. You wrote me: "If you are certain there will be no stoppage from the Ministry of Interior, I would go ahead and make the contract. One way or another, I will get the money." But how could I be sure about the Ministry of Interior?

You also wrote: "You should have complete authority to make decisions on the project. My job over here is, realistically, responsibility for the funds, and perhaps being an adviser for specific problems. But you are there, you know the needs and issues." I appreciated your confidence, but I would have hated to make a mistake with your money.

Speaking of Thanksgiving, our first in Sardinia, this turned out to be a high point. We had everyone over at our apartment for dinner. Lisa wrote to her folks:

> It was really a job to get ready. Angela and I worked solidly in the kitchen from early morning. Had a big turkey the refugees had ordered from a nearby farm. Made a very good dressing with pounds of chestnuts, one of Sardinia's plentiful products. Potatoes we mashed with our hands as we had no masher. Five bottles of wine and plenty of good food. After supper a carpenter in our apartment building brought over his gramophone, an antique with a huge brass horn, along with many dance records. We had a tremendous evening, dancing tangos, polkas. Mario was talking a blue streak about his favorite operas. He sang (sobbed) Neapolitan songs in true Gigli fashion. Giles played folk songs on his guitar and we all sang.

As the weeks edged toward Christmas, I felt the project moving forward. I had little doubt regarding the economic possibilities; if given a chance, we'd make money. And I expected to have governmental permissions eventually. But then there were the refugees. The last weeks before Christmas were difficult. Harold asked Tony to do something and Tony smacked him in the face. Harold, a conscientious objector, didn't fight back, so Giles had to fend him off. The next day I called a meeting, which lasted from 2:30 to 6:00 p.m. I said, "We are going to hang together or hang separately." The refugees and Americans were very frank. After considerable tension the meeting broke up in a rather genial spirit. The next day everyone worked harder than ever.

Since we were selling artichokes, our joint group decided that there should be a dividend totaling 100,000 lire. Each refugee would receive a sum according to his workdays. Tony asked for 100,000 lire just for himself, in order to get new teeth, glasses and clothes; he was so furious that he took no dividend. Roubal insisted he needed a sizable sum to support his family of five back in the camp. And so it went. No one could understand why the United Nations and Italian Government were not already providing money, and why Don Murray and other rich Americans didn't give everything that was needed.

I arranged for the four refugees to return to camp for a two-week Christmas break. They could get a physical exam, see friends, and Roubal could be with his family. As we put them on the boat, they were all sweetness and light, with flowery speeches of repentance. Mario asked emotionally: "How is it possible for people like you to accept and help people like us?"

Our little American group speculated: Will we ever see them again? Are they planning to come back? You wrote me, Don, a great letter, saying the project did not have to live up to our highest expectations. Should it fail, we did not fail. In any event, you planned to visit us in Sardinia in January. My wise mother in Oak Park wrote a sympathetic letter: "The project has not been going long enough to provide any sense of success or failure. Even though sometimes you think the refugees are hopeless, you are doing this project because you have faith in them. They are God's children. Don and Hope have jeopardized their whole security and reputations, as have you, and the faith of all of you will win in the end."

On January 6, the refugees came back from camp. They had talked up the project there, which led to their bringing two new members: Martinez, a Spaniard, and Marcic, a Serb. Soon after their arrival, with everyone full of exuberant energy, I called a meeting so that together we could make the next big jump in planning the future. We began by stating our goal: every person would be helped to go out on his own as soon as possible. Living collectively was untenable. We'd work hard to complete preparation of the land so that each family wishing to move into agriculture could receive a tract of three to six hectares, depending on family size. They would have a house. Families entering small industries—the concrete block business and poultry—would receive half a hectare for a home and garden.

Each person needed to think about preferences, so that by spring we could move ahead. We also discussed our linkage to the local community. Each person would find a constructive way to interact with someone in Simaxis. Each refugee would continue to receive 5,000 lire per month for food, plus dividends when there were any.

Two days later you arrived. You were very impressed by our progress; after my reports you expected far worse. You seemed all fired up to get home and raise more money. M.R. Ziegler, head of the Brethren in Geneva, who knew what all the agencies in Europe were doing, told us: "This is the most exciting project that I know of today." While these comments were overblown, they were good for our fragile egos. I got a little program going in the priest's theater, and almost the whole town came out. You and I and Piero each gave short talks. There were ballads and songs by local musicians, Harold and the boys in the 4-H club he'd organized showed you their work. Of course, the mayor and priest were delighted to meet you. A reporter came to interview you for local television.

Later, you and I took the overnight boat from Olbia to Rome. We found time to confer with the various agencies, meet James Zellerbach, the American ambassador to Italy, and visit two refugee camps. We found increasing enthusiasm for the project, although most of the authorities still had doubts as to whether the refugees would make it.

When I returned to Sardinia, I found the refugees in good spirits. Electricity had arrived onto the property, our first artichokes were so big and tasty they sold at an unheard of price. We'd produced several thousand concrete blocks for the first home and the chicken house. New refugees had arrived, Milosevic and Princic—two Serbs. It was becoming clear that the project's first phase was nearly finished. Soon we'd begin considering how to divide up the property, encouraging each refugee to go out on his own.

Since this was a key juncture, I invited Miss Buoncuore to Sardinia to get her assessment of our next steps. While she had always been supportive, after her three-day visit she was enthusiastic. She said she'd write a report to the UNHCR and Italian authorities, strongly endorsing what we were doing. She thought our experience was a model for the actual rehabilitation of refugees and she'd propose that the U.N. establish a rehabilitation fund for a center like ours, maybe using HELP as a model/mentor.

However, the project was now desperate for funds. Whenever Professor Pau passed by our house to collect his money, I became invisible. Dr. Sanna promised significant subsidies for our various developments, but they would not arrive until after each activity was completed, such as a built house or poultry facility. The United Nations promised money for each refugee after final integration. I had not heard from you for almost a month since your visit. Naturally, the refugees were complaining about why we weren't moving faster. They said you were still their friend, but "all that money you were raising in America" should have arrived by now. They expected that we, not they themselves, would determine their future, as if we held a magic wand.

Now, you arranged a near miracle. You convinced NBC to get us on national television. The popular weekly program, *This Is Your Life*, relied on the element of shock. Usually a celebrity was picked, lured to the studio, and stories of his or her life recounted. In this case, you and Hope and various members of my family (including Lisa) and friends were featured, and I, drawn from the front lines of a historic world problem, was the program's "victim." Jim Read, Deputy U.N. High Commissioner for Refugees, was flown in from Geneva, and strongly applauded our efforts. Thirty million people viewed the program and we raised over $80,000.

I returned immediately to Sardinia while Lisa stopped in Schenectady for a brief visit with her parents. A horror ensued; almost immediately, she came down with a very severe case of serum hepatitis, undoubtedly caused by our local doctor with the dirty needles to confront her boils. She was hospitalized for weeks, unable to come back to Sardinia for almost seven months. Our home-helper, Angela, and I took care of Eric until, after four months, you came to the rescue. You flew to Sardinia and brought him back to his mother.

The project experienced significant progress in the spring and summer of 1958. More refugees moved to Sardinia from the camps, we began allocating the land and set up more small industries. Another young American volunteer, John Earle Hutchinson, joined us.

Then several crises hit. Torrential rains brought massive flooding, and a quarter of our land was under water. Then Martinez, one of our healthiest and most productive refugees, almost died. He vomited blood all one night and two others stayed with him, expecting he might not make it. The next day we took him to the hospital and learned he had a stomach ulcer and had lost half his red corpuscles. A refugee and a friend in Simaxis donated a bottle of blood. An earlier incident had involved Mario. When he first came to Sardinia, he had overworked ferociously in the block business and had begun coughing blood. The refugees had stood around and watched us mop up the mess. Mario told us his real reason for joining the project was to literally work himself to death; he had no reason to live. Now, with Martinez, everyone pitched in to provide care and clean up, Mario also providing leadership. They were beginning to feel they were no longer refugees, alone in the world, bitter and suspicious. They had become "regular people," and part of a little community.

In July we hosted an international work camp organized by the Quakers. There were 28 volunteers from 14 countries. We also invited several young people from Simaxis, opening them up to the wider world, everyone working with the refugees in agriculture and construction. Since we had just completed our first refugee home and the chicken house, I used this opportunity to stage an inauguration ceremony. We invited many dignitaries, including Dr. Schlatter, head of UNHCR in Italy, other refugee authorities, representatives of the various development agencies, plus political, civic, and religious leaders.

Dr. Schlatter spoke:

> Why would a representative of the U.N. High Commissioner participate in a celebration of a rather modest undertaking? This is why: it is a pilot project, an important experiment. It will be an example to follow if the results prove to be convincing. . . . The UNHCR will do everything possible to help assure the success of this project. In a country like Italy it is nearly impossible for refugees to achieve integration and find work. . . . Here, an enterprise is being created which can serve as a model for the world.

During the next year, our regular letters continued to flow back and forth. There were high points and small crises. Some refugees settled permanently, three married local women and produced children. Others, after spending rehabilitation time with us, were able to emigrate. Few people knew that for many months you and I operated a project that had no legal existence. It was just the two of us, although the Brethren Service Commission, based in Elgin, Illinois, handled all of our American contributions as a non-profit organization. Finally, in order to receive money from Italian agencies and the United Nations, we had to create a legal entity under Italian law. Dr. Malfetanni helped us to form a cooperative, and we named it the Don Murray Refugee Committee.

Various authorities told us that HELP had engaged in several unprecedented operations. We were the first foreigners to buy land in Sardinia, the first to seek financing from Italian development agencies for land improvement and construction projects, and the first to receive a long-term agricultural loan from the government.

I received an invitation from Dr. Edna Weber, director of International Social Services in Geneva, to participate in a seminar in Rome with refugee leaders in Italy. Since she was considered a top authority on refugee psychology, she asked me to discuss "Resettlement of Difficult Cases." She and others reported to us that our experience was some of the most significant data anywhere for dealing with hard-core refugees. Later when I met her in Geneva, I was surprised to learn more: that we were demonstrating a new approach to show that at least some hard-core refugees could be brought back through work with love and understanding, and if there was faith placed in them. In effect, we had proved that a special kind of rehabilitation was possible. She urged us to publish our experience, which we did.

The UNHCR people and others talked about HELP as if we were a large organization, well staffed and financed. They needed time to absorb that this whole endeavor was just you and me and a small team of young American volunteers, and that in a few months we'd all be leaving. Miss Buonocuore couldn't believe this; she hadn't known that our original commitment was for two years. She predicted that the project might collapse.

During a Geneva trip, you spoke to the High Commissioner and other officials urging that UNHCR take a major role and figure out how to keep us directly involved. In fact, they wanted to expand the project. In early July 1959, two high UNHCR officials—Thomas Jamieson, director of operations and Jean Heidler, head of planning—visited Sardinia, along with Dr. Schlatter. Jamieson, a realist with years of experience, thought that our project might still fail. But he said it was the only project anywhere demonstrating that these refugees were capable of self-sufficiency. He took his hat off to us as "individuals with the creative spirit to undertake the impossible." He said he'd be failing in his job if he did not support us.

UNHCR hired me to serve in its Rome office as camp clearance coordinator for Italy, while also continuing to advise with Sardinia. The Brethren hired a new director with a new, small staff. In my two years with the UNHCR, I assisted in designing a plan to reorganize the Sardinia project for major expansion; it could be one solution for general camp clearance. UNHCR was ready to commit significant new resources for this purpose. For myriad political reasons, though, this plan did not materialize.

Lisa and Eric moved with me to Rome, where our second son, Steve, was born. In this period you, Don, had the misfortune that evoked huge emotional reverberations for all of us—your split with Hope. While your flourishing acting career experienced ups and downs, you continued to find creative outlets for your talents. When my family and I returned to America, I finished the Ph.D. and then joined the faculty of the University of Wisconsin.

Years later I returned to Sardinia with Lisa and our boys. We know that you also went back. The Brethren staff, which stayed on for six more years after we left, had long since turned the property over to the refugees. We spent most of our visit with Mario, Martinez and Vinko, all of whom had married local women, had children, and had integrated economically. In 2014 the mayor of Simaxis invited you and me to return and to make us honorary citizens of the town. You went over for this with your sons, and the whole town showed up for a gala event. Now, after more than half a century, this ceremonial commemoration was recognizing the local significance of the HELP experiment. The refugees were all dead, but their wives and children lived on. You continue to correspond with Mayor Cossu, and I with Vinko's daughter, Vlada.

As I reflect on our entire experience with HELP, I ask the question: What does it take to accept the challenge of tackling a significant world need when we ourselves are relatively powerless as individuals, with meager resources? One must think big. One's ideals and energy must attempt to bridge the gap between the lofty vision and the likely reality that achieving the vision may be nearly impossible. Most folks moderate their dreams of taking on such formidable tasks, unwilling to risk likely failure. As a result, the status quo prevails, critical problems remain unsolved. The experience of the two of us with HELP represents one tiny authentic example of a couple of idealists, with their small company of colleagues, marshaling the courage to shoot for a very difficult outcome. This was our way of saying that we were accepting a big risky challenge, and that, no matter what happened, we believed we could achieve something positive, even the impossible.

Italian ex-communist Athos Ricci
pushes reform with traditional values

Caro Athos,

I was told I had to meet you before leaving Rome. It was said you were brilliant. You had made your town one of the most communist-voting towns in all of Italy. Since this was the early 1960s, at the height of the Cold War when Italy might go communist in free elections, your experience had more than passing international significance.

When I met you the first time in your town outside Rome I thought this would be a one-time visit. It was toward the end of my assignment with the U.N. High Commissioner for Refugees, and I'd begun to think about returning to America to rewrite my Ph.D. thesis and then find a job. As I've learned again and again, however, unexpected encounters become key juncture points that change predetermined routes.

You had just left the Italian Communist Party. You were full of why you had left; you were disillusioned, your ideals were being wasted. You were not sure if you wanted to be seen talking to an American. Before we entered your house you glanced around to make sure that no one was within earshot.

You had joined the Party at the urging of your older brother, Federico. He had given heroic leadership in organizing the Resistance against Mussolini's fascism in the area. After the Nazis took over in the war, they hunted for him and he was almost captured several times. At that point the communists stood for radical change—Federico saw the Party as the vanguard for creating a new Italy after the war.

I'd first heard about you when I happened to meet the editor of a political journal in the library of the Christian Democrat Party in Rome. Since he knew my interest in village communism, he said, "Before you go home you must visit Genazzano and meet Athos Ricci." A few days later the two of us escaped the sweltering heat of Rome to take a delightful trek out to your countryside. At that elevation the evening was cool as we strolled through the vineyards clustered on the hillsides. We could see the outline of the medieval castle still guarding the walled town of several thousand souls.

You had trained in the communist schools that prepared local leaders, with the goal of bringing communism to the villages. You were so successful that Genazzano was seen as a national model. Your town became known as "Little Moscow."

Although now rabidly *anti*-communist, you still had fire in your eyes. In contrast to leaders of other parties I'd met, money and career did not dominate your interest. You made clear why people found it almost impossible to leave the Party. It took courage to join, to be threatened in every way and intimidated by employers, but once in, you had a mission.

After this first encounter, you said we needed to meet again. As your suspicion of me subsided, you became more and more friendly and expansive. You gave me a valuable windfall: a set of 12 booklets used by the Party to train leaders and activists. They dealt with the communist view of man and society, the nature of capitalist society, war and peace, and problems on the village level directed to specific audiences, such as the youth and farmers. And of course they played up the relationship of the Party to the USSR—"the paradise of the world." I found nothing comparable in my research on the other parties, including the Christian Democrats who were supported by the American government. Later, I showed your material to my good friend at the American Embassy, John Baker, the assistant political attaché. He was surprised at its comprehensiveness and sophistication.

You suggested that we do an analysis of three nearby villages that had similar conditions but with very different political complexions. One was Christian Democrat, one fascist, and then your communist Genazzano.

You said it made no sense for me to commute every day from Rome to Genazzano, an hour by car or two hours by a bus that stopped at every town. Since there were no hotels in Genazzano, you said: "Let's try the friars." You were referring to the Irish Augustinian monastery called San Pio, located high on a promontory outside the village. I met the rector, Father Duffner, an affable, shrewd Irishman. He had 30 priests, Irish and American, studying at the Jesuit Gregorian University in Rome. During the warm months they lived at San Pio.

Father Duffner said the priests had no contact with the village and it would be tragic if when they'd completed their studies and had fanned out into the world, that they knew nothing about communism. "Let's make a deal. I'll give you a cell and subsistence at no cost. In return, you'll eat with the students when you're around and share with them what you are learning about the village."

Fair enough.

You remember my cell on the second floor in this austere stone building. It was constructed by the early Romans and used by the emperors to get away from the summer heat of Rome. I had a narrow cot with a crucifix above, a table for my typewriter, and a small bookcase. There was a bathroom down a long corridor with toilets and cold showers. While the place was poorly maintained, it was famous for its spectacular view overlooking the valley, and also its medieval frescoes of saints and prophets. Sometimes you'd take over a nearby cell and we'd draw in folks from around town to talk for hours. Every morning we inspected our shoes for scorpions.

I found the priests spiritual, but also playful to the extreme. We fraternized not only at mealtime but also in the monastery's swimming pool. We conversed over the delicious white wine produced in the well-tended vineyards. I imagined monks of the past in these ancient monasteries who contributed some of the world's great scholarship. I could picture Genazzano then, this town founded in 1053 with its medieval castle, presided over for centuries by the Prince Colonna family. They controlled this whole sub-region and produced several popes.

After Lisa and our two sons, Eric and Steve, left Rome for the U.S., we agreed that I'd stay on to finish up with the UNHCR. Dr. Beerman, our Italy director, asked me to work part-time for several more months. I now felt this assignment combined nicely with my new commitment with you in Genazzano. In Rome, after we gave up our house, I stayed with a friend from the Associated Press, and when in Genazzano, I was at San Pio.

It had been a good while since I'd thought much about my Ph.D. thesis and my advisor, Professor Finer. Before I left for Sardinia in latter 1957 to embark on the refugee project with Don Murray, Finer had told me that the first draft of my thesis was unacceptable. He made crystal clear that my topic—the role of non-governmental agencies in international relations—was interesting but not political science. It would require major surgery. Now, four years later, I had a tantalizing idea: chuck my unacceptable thesis subject. Grab a sure-fire theme that would appeal to Finer, who was interested in Italian politics, especially Mussolini's fascism. My focus would be Italian communism. My research would center on a case study of Genazzano, conducted in partnership with you, my invaluable guide. I would pay you something for your help, but as a writer you'd be most interested if eventually we could convert our work together into a published book.

Before continuing this letter to you on our collaboration in Genazzano, I want to add a few lines about what was happening as I was wrapping up my work with UNHCR. Since one of my primary responsibilities was to continue to support the refugee project in Sardinia where Don Murray and I had invested our creative energies in recent years, I'll summarize recent developments. Don and I passed the administration of HELP over to the Brethren Service Commission, which appointed a new director, John Barwick, to replace me. Subsequently, he was replaced by Ellis Schenk. UNHCR advanced some money, and later the project received substantial financing from the Italian development agencies and the Italian Department of Agriculture.

As Camp Clearance Coordinator with the U.N., my job was to help in figuring out how to close all the refugee camps in Italy. I assisted in designing a broad policy that included substantial expansion of the Sardinia project. This would include significant financial backing from the U.N. and the Italian Government, but it also required major reorganization of the project. The Brethren, however, decided not to accept this plan. HELP itself, therefore, continued as a small-scale pilot effort. Its experience confirmed our original goal of resettling a number of the refugees we knew, and most importantly, it contributed to broad policy-making. Of course, Don and I greatly regretted that the expansion approved by the governmental authorities did not happen.

One larger application I also worked on was to discuss with the U.N. and authorities in the Near East various ways to utilize what we had learned in Sardinia, e.g. to organize a pilot effort with Palestinian refugees. Since they had been stagnating for years in camps and suffered psychological problems similar to the refugees we knew, our experience could be relevant. And the strategy we designed that combined economic development with refugee resettlement could be adapted for refugees leaving the camps to be integrated elsewhere in the Near East. There was considerable correspondence and discussion with various authorities but no further action that I was involved with.

Today there are millions of refugees in the world needing solutions. Their plight was brought about by wars, persecution, and impacts of natural catastrophes and climate change, far more complex problems than in the period when Don Murray and I were working in Italy. While I am no longer active with this situation, our Sardinia project experience continues to offer valuable ideas. Many of today's refugees spend years in camps and the "refugee psychology" remains a prominent issue. The main resettlement solutions will probably not be emigration to other countries but integration into the regions themselves through creative development projects such as our Sardinia example.

There is one other result of our HELP project. Both Don Murray and I continued to have contact with our U. S. senator, Hubert Humphrey; from our early days of project planning he had been intrigued by our efforts and at one time almost visited us in Sardinia. Directly after John Kennedy was elected president, Humphrey told Don that our experience with young Americans creatively grappling with major unsolved world problems was one factor that stimulated Kennedy to establish the Peace Corps under Sargent Shriver. Lisa and I also learned that Gordon Boyce, the director of the Experiment in International Living, had given to Shriver (a personal friend) my proposal on "Soldiers of Understanding." This would utilize young Americans selected to work in dangerous areas of conflict to create conditions for peaceful solutions.

Returning to our Genazzano experience, every day I would hike down from the monastery into the town and surrounding fields and valleys and hills. You were my guide and ever-present companion, the most astute and informed person in Genazzano. Then in your early thirties, you'd finished only eight grades of formal schooling, but you read the classics, wrote poetry and plays, and composed music for your guitar. You were equally at home with an illiterate farmer in his field or a visiting celebrity.

You had the most penetrating comprehension of the traditional rural culture that was based in agriculture and craftsmanship in the building trade. By nature the farmers were conservative yet were struggling for a more prosperous life. You understood the historic weight of poverty and injustice and the key issues to be addressed to bring about change. You were wary of simply throwing out the old for rapid material wellbeing—the communist doctrine. You knew the subtleties: the village had certain precious qualities to be preserved, such as closeness to the earth, cohesive families, and interests that went deeper than the material. Your goal was to find a compromise between the traditional and modern worlds.

We spent hours together in the fields or at the monastery, or strolling through the narrow, winding cobblestone streets in the village to your house, the rustic but elegant stone structure your father had built. Whenever I sat down at your place, your lovely, traditional wife, Giuseppina, brought out a mouth-watering mountain of spaghetti with a liter of local *vino*. When eating, your total focus was on that process and you stopped talking. I could sense you were savoring the whole meal experience, as if enveloped in an ancient ritual, which, try as I might, I would never fully understand.

Since you lived at home, I saw a good bit of your family. Your father had served in the elite forces, the *bersaglieri*, at the World War I front where he lost a leg. Despite his peg leg, he was surprisingly dexterous as he plied his trade as a mason and builder. Basically apolitical, he had nothing good to say about any politician of any stripe. He returned from the war a hero, and because the fascists could not touch him during the 20 years of Mussolini's era, he became a rallying point for people resisting fascism. As an untainted civic leader at the end of World War II, the Allies selected him as the town's interim mayor.

Your older brother, Federico, like your father, was a first-class craftsman who built and restored houses in Rome. After his fierce wartime resistance against the fascists and Nazis, he continued to be an idealistic communist. He knew and still socialized with the Party's inner circle, and given his past, it seems they respected his independence. Unlike you, he never left the Party although he was very aware of its narrow, power-driven goals. Your other brother was a well-known artist based in Rome, showing in many international exhibitions. Though left-leaning, his commissions came from clients of all persuasions.

Apart from yourself, my most intense talks with your family were with Federico. He was very astute. Even though aware of how the Party had prostituted its one-time idealism, he saw that for him withdrawal would mean entering a spiritual vacuum. I sensed that you, too, had entered a spiritual desert, but somehow you found some solace, not in the political opposition—such as the so-called democratic Christian Democrat Party—but more through identifying with the internal pulse of the village, the deeply grounded historic culture that was now in danger of being lost.

As you and I immersed ourselves, day after day, in the life of the town, we uncovered an incredibly rich mosaic of characters. Genazzano had had its share of brutal experiences during the decades of fascism. There were Black Shirts, mostly unskilled and often illiterate, but given unbridled power, they ravaged the town as bullies and thugs. We spent considerable time with several of them. The First World War had moved a number of young men from the town to the northern front. When they returned there were no job possibilities except for unskilled farm work. The town produced a notable who became a fascist consul in the province, and also a general in Rome.

Maggiore Patriottini now lived in retirement in a small, attractive *villetta* off the main *piazza*. The tables and walls of his home conspicuously displayed relics and photographs of distinguished fascists and their exploits. There are snapshots of him in the trenches with Mussolini. As the town's most important living dignitary, he was eager to talk to me, not at all cowed by the current communist reign, as were many in the opposition. He considered the communists low-class riffraff, a sad comedown from the well-ordered spit-and-polish of Mussolini's 20 years. He didn't participate in Mussolini's famous March on Rome in 1922, but a number of men from the town did. He was arrested in 1945 and said that twice he was taken before a firing squad by the Partisans and each time they executed others around him but spared him. He said he was subjected to endless persecutions and drained financially, but was not condemned for anything.

He said in the beginning fascism was democratic, but after the liberals and socialists left parliament, strong government took over—bringing more order and discipline. Most of the time, local citizens were controlled by the ruling class, mainly lawyers and businessmen. He said the present communist leaders were once fascists, including the present mayor, who "licked his boots." He said he admired the four or five anti-fascists who held to their convictions to the end (including your father). The *squadristi*, the local Black Shirts, kept order. One of the best known of these was Nerone Pugnaloni, a "historic figure" in Genazzano.

We found Pugnaloni in the poor quarter of the village, his shack bare and dirty. Most of the local Black Shirts came from the proletariat. They were not tied to the land, had no essential skills. Pugnaloni served on the front line of the assault troops in the war. Even as he gestured and talked across the table, I could feel his crude strength and violence. When he banged his fist, the table shuddered. We finished a liter, or rather he did, of cheap *vino rosso*. He remained a fanatic fascist, while others of his social class—the semi-skilled manual workers—became communists. He said that while most of the time he was a house painter, his greatest accomplishment was as a Black Shirt.

He and his brother organized the March on Rome from Genazzano—40 men. He carried a pistol, and others had rifles and daggers. "Our objective was to keep the government from falling to the communists," he said. "In Genazzano we had 75 Black Shirts. When there was anti-fascist action in town, we would fight over who would mete out the punishment." There was both cooperation and tension between their fascist militia and the national police, the *carabinieri*. "When we had brawls with the communists, sometimes we and the communists ended up in jail together. I must have been arrested 30 times." He was convinced that "it's just a question of a few years until fascism comes back. All we need is a leader with Mussolini's strength."

Athos, as I write to you, today's Italy is not unlike past years: unstable governments continually changing, an economy barely functioning, and huge unemployment among the youth (many of whom are highly educated). The fascist party is small, but Livio Berlusconi—a figure with similar tendencies—took control for years until his many personal illegal adventures forced him and his party out of power. And it's said that today, even with his advancing age, his party might come back.

Today in Western Europe the populist uproar against the hundreds of thousands of migrants from the Middle East is challenging moderate leaders and the continuation of the European Community that has preserved democratic institutions since the Second World War. Currently, the media attention Donald Trump is attracting with his "strong leader" model, similar to that of Recep Tayyip Erdogan in Turkey, begin to have a familiar ring. Does all this sound something like Italy in the 1920s and Germany in the early 1930s? In years past, at first there were simply cries for strong democratic leadership to respond to dysfunctional government, which soon descended into authoritarian systems. The Patriottinis and Pugnalonis of Italy in those decades may not be as distant as the calendar suggests.

With the end of World War II and the death of fascism, a new order was emerging in Italy. On the local level in towns such as Genazzano, there was a small group that had demonstrated courage and energy in the Resistance movement, and was probably the most understanding of the new realities. They were aware of the decline of the old aristocracy and of a new vacuum to be filled. You masterfully described the complete turnover of the ruling class over a couple of generations.

You noted that the first big changes had taken place in the early 19th century when the new bourgeois professional classes filled the vacuum left by the collapse of feudalism. In

Genazzano several families replaced the one family that had singlehandedly dominated this part of Italy for centuries and ruled it as a feudal fiefdom. Today the ancient Colonna family retains title of nobility and still has wealth. Streets and buildings carry its name, but it has no power. The new class had accumulated large tracts of land and with this came economic and political power. Since the latter 19th century, Italy experienced the beginnings of constitutional democracy. Power had to be exercised with increasing subtlety. The ruling families had to learn how to manipulate elections.

Of the four old families that ruled the town on the eve of World War I, Lorenzo Tramonta was the last representative still around. His children had left, and he was selling off his land, acre by acre, to pay taxes. His twin nieces still lived in Genazzano. Although relatively young, they had little or no communication with others of the new generation. They could not easily leave the town because they had no marketable skills, other than collecting rents from the remaining properties.

You and I spent hours with Tramonta because he was an articulate observer of his own fate. He gave us a classic personal glimpse of the decline of the once powerful aristocracy. I was very curious going to his villa outside of town—an imposing three-story structure resembling a Swiss chalet, with parquet floors and elegant furniture. His complex had a large barn and other outbuildings, including a machine shed with ancient tractors. There was livestock all around: cattle, hogs, chickens, ducks, and turkeys. We sensed an illusive air of past luxury, but now the estate was clearly rundown. The long winding drive up from the main paved road was lined with hedges and trees, but the hedges were untrimmed and the weeds choking. All the buildings needed paint and repair.

Tramonta was an imposing figure, over six feet tall. He still had the air of a *signore*. He opened several bottles of the best wine he produced. It was cold and smooth—perfect for this hot July afternoon. He said that once he and his contemporaries leave the scene, no one will know firsthand "what the old days were like," when all the farmers bowed to him as he went to church on Sunday morning, when he could pay or not pay his landless tenants their paltry wage without concern for worker protests. Although lacking formal university education, he was a man of culture, was well traveled and politically sophisticated. His speech was strong and measured until he exploded on certain subjects, such as his downfall and the cultural poverty of the new *classe dirigente* (ruling class) that replaced his own at the end of World War II.

As the three of us sat together I felt we were witnessing history—you and Tramona were both ill at ease with the other. You were a man of the people, comfortable in the local bars where you knew everyone, you were a sensitive student and participant of the changing world. You were without large resources but with a huge grasp of the ancient regimes and of fascism, communism, and democracy. His family, in contrast, inherited large tracts of land in the early 18th century and completely controlled the economics and politics of the area up until fascism in the 20s. They made peace with the fascist state by commanding the militia in the region. Finally, when the Allies came through in 1943, Tramonta was arrested, temporarily jailed, had no power, no friends, and could barely survive on his dwindling estate.

Tramonta understood his downfall, but only vaguely the larger context. "We have fallen, these several old families with land, and nobody has replaced us, or rather the people who replaced us do not have the ability to govern. They respected us out of fear, but not affection. The old upper class simply looked out for its own interests and kept telling itself, 'There is nothing to worry about.' We didn't encourage anyone to like us; in fact, we made the townspeople hate us. The most serious mistake we made was at the end of the second war. In the postwar period we had a deathly fear of re-entering political life in Genazzano. We could not face the mob out in the *piazza* or at the ballot box. When we withdrew, others stepped forward."

More and more, as we listened to Tramonta lament the mistakes of his class, I thought of our own "ruling class" today in the United States. It is not a landed aristocracy, but some would say it is a controlling elite, greedy and insensitive. Today's Italian "aristocracy" uses the democratic system in different ways than did Tramonta and his contemporaries, but perhaps the results are not too dissimilar. It uses money to win elections and manipulate public opinion, not only in the local towns but to gain control over the national government. The resulting inequality is not as stark as in Tramonta's day, but it clearly exists and significant changes will result.

Athos, you kept insisting that I should spend still more time with your brother. I knew Federico had long ago formed stereotypes about America and Americans. He had absorbed all the propaganda that Americans are capitalists, supporters of the rigid status quo in Italian society over which they try to preside. Americans are vehemently dedicated to the overthrow of communism, including Italian communism. While he had tried to avoid me, assuming I was a lackey of the Department of State or CIA, I had one advantage: you were my collaborator.

Although younger and now outside the Party, you'd been close to Federico all your life. You knew the intimate details of his war experiences and his genuine interest in social justice—that he was a true idealist. If he were really to open up, he'd give a rare glimpse, more profound than from any book, as to how communism took hold in Italy after the war, and why it's so difficult even for an idealist to leave the Party. We'd see America's stupidities in dealing with communism throughout the world. You promised Federico that I had no official connections with the American government, staying in the monastery in order to be close to the town, that I was here to learn about communism from an authentic voice.

Finally we met at your simple apartment in Rome on a hot summer evening. As we entered, I noticed in the murky shadows a young man with a beard—we called him Barbetta. It was quickly apparent that he was Federico's counselor and control/check. He was the son of a top-echelon communist leader and he would be a "witness" should any murmurs come out that Party "confidences" were being given to an American. You brought out a few liters of red wine, recently poured from a Genazzano wine cellar, and a basket of freshly roasted chicken. After some opening minutes when Federico threw out a barb or two about American stupidities in foreign policy and how probably he was wasting his time talking to an American, and Barbetta was nervously stroking his beard, we got going. We kept going for four hours until his narrative was slowed by drowsiness. Barbetta had long since lost interest, convinced I was no Embassy spy.

I had a tape recorder and here's the gist of what he told us:

How did I get the idea of being an anti-fascist? My father never mentioned politics at home. His anti-fascism was born of protest. I was subtly influenced, until I developed attitudes and rebellion and anger against the whole constituted order, the status quo. My father fought at the front in the first war. A grenade tore off his left leg in one clean blast. He was nearly buried alive, they wrapped him in a sheet to throw him into a ditch, but a chaplain saved him.

In 1918 he returned to Genazzano and saw the whole process of fascism being born. He never belonged to any political party. His revolt against fascism was one of conscience. His feelings were shared by a number of local artisans—especially the *muratori*—who were skilled, self-employed bricklayers. They were in revolt against all the vestiges of medieval life in the town. The more alert and progressive people—mainly the construction workers and a few small farmers—began to see that fascism was simply an effort to rebuild the power of the Colonna family and Tramonta. Some of this anti-fascist faction became more and more political and eventually were called communists, a communism still primitive with romantic overtones. This rudimentary unity that began in the 1920s became a precious heritage during the critical days of the *Resistenza* when we were fighting the Germans and the most ferocious fascists near the end of the war.

All of the middle-sized and large landholders, plus the richest people in Genazzano, were fascist, while a good percentage of the artisans were anti-fascist. Other fascists were the *declassate*, people like Pugnaloni. They were unskilled workers and shepherds who were fooled into believing that fascism would help them. The *squadristi* came from their ranks. Most of the small farmers were politically apathetic—not anti-fascist but simply non-fascist, and they were Catholic. The clergy of Genazzano during all 20 years of fascism remained passive.

Our anti-fascism began little by little to take on a political form. We were not only against the regime; the protest was a rebellion against the oppression of a feudal social system. Our political forces began as a generalized anti-fascist resistance, then took on a kind of romantic socialism, vaguely against all the evils of the older order, and finally developed into communism. Real contact with the Party came with the war, around 1942, when I was a soldier. A number of times I had a chance to travel to Russia, serving as an escort on troop trains. Upon returning from one of these trips I took on the job of forming a Communist Party in Genazzano. There was need for a stable, secure leadership. When the Armistice was announced in 1943, the members assembled to be given their first duties.

They did not have long to wait. On leaving the meeting, the comrades were attacked in the main *piazza* by a band of the town's most violent fascists. Several communists were arrested and put in prison. The next day the Germans occupied the town. People were urged to continue fighting the fascists and Germans. The Armistice simply ended the war against the Allies. The Germans were well informed about the anti-fascists and communists organizing the Resistance, and it was only a miracle that I escaped the SS. Now the true battle against fascism began.

An extraordinary event occurred: a small group of Americans parachuted into our territory to stir up trouble against the Germans, and I joined them. I was given American weapons and a radio transmitter to signal the American army about local German military targets. The material was dropped in the ditch near the monastery. I used the top of the monastery bell tower for radio signaling. Our little sub-region was the center of the only organized resistance in the general area, and it was composed almost entirely of communists.

The Allied occupation of Genazzano after the flight of the Germans was directed by the Canadians, presided over by an Englishman. My father became the first mayor, and then other mayors were picked until the first elections in 1946. Right after the liberation almost everyone wanted to join the Communist Party. The interim mayors were all communist but the Christian Democrat Party was reconstituted in the Catholic parishes. The priests handed down orders to win the first election. In the neighboring villages communism all but disappeared with one exception: Genazzano. Here there were a few individuals who knew how to create and sustain an ideal and organize into a political party. They had demonstrated an alternative during fascism and they had analyzed local conditions more profoundly than anyone else.

We had our problems too. For example, a group of communist vagrants had attacked a bar with hand grenades and a submachine gun, only because the owner had been a fascist. All hell broke out because peaceful citizens were caught in the middle of the fray. This kind of thing didn't help us. Then there was stupid discrimination against relatives of Black Shirts. It was a politics of vendetta.

One or two fascists left town, never to return. The others we turned over to the Allies; they spent a few months in prison camps, nothing more. But when they came home they were cut off from most of the town. Also, the old families, like Tramonta, were completely isolated from the population. Our political fight now would be strictly against the Christian Democrats. Apart from the first election in 1946, the most critical moment in our postwar politics was in 1948. The Christian Democrats mobilized all their forces in Genazzano, as they did nationally. Their electoral campaign was not simply political; it was a terrorist offensive loosed by the clergy. The sole motive was anti-communism, and the refrain was that the Americans—who were keeping Italy alive then—would suspend all aid if the communists won.

We made very important use of the struggle over uncultivated land. In 1947-48 the farmers, under communist inspiration, appropriated much of the unused land, and this completely changed the financial position of the peasantry. Poverty-stricken day laborers now became successful farmers.

The Communist Party has survived in postwar Italy and in Genazzano. But it has not all been wine and roses. Take my own personal situation. I never became mayor; I lack the ability for intrigue and compromise. I have spent my adult life fighting degeneration. I firmly opposed a politics of blood for blood. My job was more delicate than being mayor; I was the responsible communist official for the whole zone. Throwing oneself into a fight for greater social justice depends on one's own character. You must be fired up by an ideal. The Party is what it is today only because of the spirit generated by the inner group of dedicated workers. But these idealists—the ones who sit up late in cafes—are not monolithic. More than a few of us have nearly left the Party. The Party today is full of fakers who are not men of character. If our Party is to take power, it needs the re-commitment of its members who too often have become old and lazy. We need men of culture—"complete men," not just *funzionari* (bureaucrats). A good example of Party hypocrisy is the present mayor of Genazzano, who has been in office for more than a decade. He had been a fanatic fascist but switched in 1948. He has never gone through the purifying process of self-criticism.

I suppose you want to know why I don't leave the Party and go elsewhere? Why do we idealists, although sometimes disillusioned and embittered, seldom leave the Party? The question is not simple. There are a number of key strata in the Party. The *dirigenti verticali*, the top leadership, have spent their entire life inside the Party. Most have known prison and sacrifice. Today they view communism as something infallible. They have seen growth from a tiny group to a quarter of the electorate. They've become largely incapable of critical self-examination.

The *quadri intermedi*, the middle echelons, are, above all, careerists. They are capable of any intrigue; they're as mediocre as they are conformist. But communism gives them a job and prestige they're unlikely to find anywhere else. This would define our Genazzano mayor. Then there are the *uomini di cultura*, the men of culture. Most Italian intellectuals are of the political Left. Part of this is snobbery; they have the image of being the conscience of Italian society. The communists have made it fashionable to criticize the government, the clergy, and *la dolce vita*. They are genuine critics of the status quo. They have a natural home with us. Where else would they have to go?

We cannot forget *il ceto medio*, the middle class, which every year becomes more important in Italy. This class lives in the shadow of a thousand fears—bankruptcy, taxes, political failure. It wants only to be on the winning side. The greatest fear of the bourgeoisie was always socialism or communism, but in Genazzano communists are their good friends.

You see the tremendous differences among these groups. They all have their deficits; there is more self-interest than idealism. They all have one thing in common: they stay in the Communist Party or at least remain sympathetic to it. Who knows how many times I've thought about the contradictions within our movement and want to send everybody to the devil! But how could I forget the horrors of fascism and the Nazis, my father's protests, my *compagni* with whom I fought in the Resistance, a lifetime of insults. We are all gladiators. The Party is like a mother who tells her beautiful fables, who demands obedience.

Communism gives a purpose. Whatever can be said against the Party, we know we are in a battle where there is no truce until the final triumph. It is easy for a non-communist who has never experienced our deep commitment to advise us to quit, but he simply doesn't understand. "Democratic parties" are strictly political; the Christian Democrats think only in terms of winning elections. But we seek a better society where there is true justice. What non-communist has experienced this kind of commitment? If the Party idealist leaves the Party, what is he going to do? There is no democratic alternative in Italy. The Christian Democrats are a corrupt electoral machine. The parties to the Right—they are unthinkable for anyone who lived under fascism. So if I leave the Party, where do I go? I enter the solitude. The comrades who have left become lonely individuals, divorced from their friends, cut off from a great ideal.

Who knows, if someday I were to find a new moral and civil honesty, new courageous missionaries to renew the world and obliterate injustice, plant a new spirit in every hamlet, I might even be converted. I am only one man, but there are thousands like me.

The more I talked to Federico, I wondered about our own politics: all the money spent, the narrow partisanship, the lack of real concern for the larger common good. It is not only in Italy; perhaps it is everywhere. Today we fight the different brands of terrorists, whether in the Middle East or elsewhere, and with good reason. There is the frequent barbarism and complete lack of humanity. But so much of the political world is made up of the *funzionari* Federico describes—the purely selfish, the opportunists. He asks, we all ask: where are the idealists whose full commitment is to build a better world?

Athos, this brings me back to you. You and Federico seldom mentioned the Soviet Union. Your communism was close to the idealism all of us share. When for several months I lived at the monastery, I became practically a part of your family. We had plenty of time to talk about our lives. Even though you had given up on communism, you were at loose ends, just as your brother had said—living in the solitude. The more I talked with your family, and many in Genazzano who called themselves communist, you were focusing on an ideal more than a political party. As Federico said, one remains communist as a commitment to a set of values. Granted, the USSR and its governmental allies in the world were a significant political and military force, and from the view of the West this had to be countered. But at the grassroots we were dealing with people who seek a better life, and it seems the Communist Party at times had been more effective in selling its ideology than the opposition. In other words, articulation of a persuasive alternative based on values had been lacking; "Democracy" was more an electoral machine than a meaningful alternative.

After our months together in summer and fall 1961, I knew you wondered if we'd ever meet again. We continued with a rather prolific correspondence. You kept sending me clippings on Italian politics. I sorted out my packs of notes and reread the documents stored in boxes I shipped home. My overwhelming goal now was to return to Professor Finer and finish my Ph.D. After my experience with HELP in Sardinia and the United Nations in Rome, I felt my original thesis on the role of non-governmental organizations in international relations was a valid subject, but Finer had argued that this was not political science. Now I'd convert my ton of material into a completely new doctoral thesis: Italian Communism.

After several months I sent Finer a draft entitled, "Revolution in the Villages of South Italy." It focused on the causes and operations of communism in the villages of poor South Italy, using details you and I had gathered in the villages, especially Genazzano. He loved it—"unusually distinguished work," he said. This made my day. A few months later in 1962, I picked up the Ph.D. Soon thereafter I was invited to join the faculty at the University of Wisconsin.

You undoubtedly recall my letter to you in fall 1963. A publisher, Ivan Dee, of Quadrangle Books, had contacted me just after talking to Professor Finer, who had told him about my thesis. Dee was fascinated and urged me to consider returning to Genazzano to gather more data for a book. I invited you to renew our collaboration for summer 1964. You wrote back with a bunch of questions, concluding, "If the scope of our study on Italian communism were to create a policy to bring economic and political change to the villages, then I will work with you."

I returned to my old cell at the San Pio monastery. I enlisted three young men, including a university graduate student from Rome, to conduct one-hour interviews with every 15th name of Genazzano's 3,000 voters. From our research of three years before, we already knew the village's central actors, and from that roster we selected 30 people to contact. You and I followed the same routine as before, visiting each person at home, at work, in a vineyard or wherever, typically planning a two-hour tape-recorded interview that sometimes went on much longer. You then took home each tape and parked at your typewriter for an average of eight hours to transcribe each tape—truly a labor of love. At the end of the summer when I returned home, there was a second labor of love. Lisa took on the massive assignment of translating all the tapes from Italian to English.

Our final product was published by Quadrangle Books in 1966. Entitled *The Searchers: Conflict and Communism in an Italian Town*, most of the 12 chapters used the verbatim taped dialogue—the authentic words of this cross-section of the village. I introduced each chapter by describing the background of the people interviewed, placing their roles into the larger story of the town and their relationship to communism. Most of the book reviews published in periodicals in the United States were favorable, although there were only modest sales.

Over most of the next decade we had little contact. Then in 1973, a half-time university sabbatical brought me back to Italy. I had a research project, to assess what had happened after 15 years to the refugees we had resettled in Sardinia. A number of them were flourishing. With Lisa and our two teenage sons, we picked up a Volkswagon Super Beetle in Luxembourg and drove around Europe, with a major stop in Sardinia and, of course, a visit with you in Genazzano. Our boys loved exploring the monastery with all its mysterious recesses, and examining the faded frescoes on the walls of this very old Roman structure.

We continued to have periodic contact. You were publishing poetry and writing articles depicting your view of the world, usually in the context of your beloved town. The same communist mayor still ran Genazzano. You still had a meaningless clerical job in Rome but spent as much time as possible in the village. I vaguely talked about bringing you to America, to visit us in Wisconsin after all your unstinting assistance with my research.

Since this period was the height of the Cold War, many folks in America were interested in our book: what was a real-life communist village like? Now and then I gave talks and wrote articles. One day in 1976 you wrote me that you had found the resources and intended to show up in America. We could discuss a new book. Naturally, I immediately responded that we'd love to see you. You flew over and stayed with us for three weeks. Since several years earlier Lisa and I had bought a 46-acre farm an hour north of our home in Milwaukee, we decided to spend some time there, figuring that you'd like to check out rural America.

As a keen observer of the United States on a first-time visit, you shared with us your first impressions after two days in Milwaukee. You'd enjoy Lisa's notes:

> Athos went for long walks (with no car, he was used to walking around the village), and was struck by the number of joggers, including women. He keeps remarking on the dour expressions of everyone, their stolid way of moving with measured, purposeful steps. He lighted up when we drove him through the black inner city sectors where crowds gathered and people were lounging on their front

steps and porches and laughing. This was more like the lighthearted, "enjoy every minute to the fullest even if you have nothing"— lifestyle he knew.

Then we drove up affluent Lake Drive, where he noted all the elaborate iron gates and ornate stone walls around the mansions. It reminded him of the cemetery in Rome—the rich buried in their palatial mausoleums. He was struck by how ordered and clean the city was, even beautiful. Too bad that nobody seemed to be enjoying it. At night, apart from the inner city, the streets were empty. He kept asking, "Where are the people?"

You remember we then moved up to our farm. You lapped it up, the simple life, the local stories about the early Indian settlements. You selected the most spartan bed in our century-old farmhouse. We took long walks through the woods. Lisa dug out a primitive espresso machine for Italian coffee. After she returned to Milwaukee, you took over cooking for the two of us: *fritatta* with vegetables all out of our garden, sauteed in olive oil, then with beaten eggs and milk poured over, like an omelet. You said the chuck steak and corn on the cob I grilled over an open fire was the best you'd ever had. The editor of the local paper interviewed you for a feature article; he pronounced you "an incredible character."

Most of the time we just talked. Now and then you'd get a flash, waking me up at 3:00 in the morning. It had been some 15 years since we first met in the early '60s. Your village was changing. In my first visits the great issue in Genazzano was *La Miseria*, the stark poverty and lack of social justice, fully exploited by the communists. Your town now was still communist, but a new dynamic had entered the picture.

The old rural civilization was suffering its death knell. Many of the young people who before couldn't wait to leave the village to seek their fortunes in Rome or other cities, had begun to trickle back. They belonged to the same vanguard as their generation in the richer countries—certainly the U.S.—those who were raising fundamental questions about modern consumer society. While in the past they had seen petty corruption in Genazzano, now they were becoming aware of big-time scandals that were making the national government dysfunctional. They saw the vast, anonymous slums on the urban periphery, which made village poverty look not so bad. At least most villagers had a plot of land to feed themselves. In the city they'd become part of the rat race, where it seemed people's goal was to make all the money they could and buy all the things they didn't need.

You knew all these young people. They had no interest in throwing out the material amenities they had acquired, but they were also looking for something more. While a part of their new rebellion was against the disorder of the big city, much of it was a deeper battle, against the new materialism. They were searching for a sense of community they knew in the village: cohesion of family, closeness to the land, the ubiquitous craftsmanship enabling people who were small-time artisans to take care of themselves without paying others to perform services for them.

In our long talks you may recall I also mentioned two events in the personal lives of Lisa and me that were to affect us long-term. The university had asked me to serve as academic director of a university-sponsored seminar in New York dealing with the United Nations. For two weeks in July I had 17 students from eight campuses around Wisconsin with me to learn about U.N. activities. I pulled in experts from many U.N. agencies for impressive debates. Much of the focus was on two hot topics in those days: the New Economic Order that emphasized the growing interdependence of the rich and poor countries, and the finiteness of world resources and the need to reassess the values of industrial civilization.

The other event, which soon would have far-reaching significance, was Lisa's three-week trip in October to the Findhorn community in Scotland. This was a famous "intentional" community committed to designing a culture based on enlightened values. It was focused on living with a deep connection to nature. The farm, where you and I were now staying by ourselves, would end up as the nucleus of an ecological community that Lisa and I soon helped to found. Based on the Findhorn idea, it would be called High Wind.

You and I kept talking about all of these issues. While we had begun to address them years earlier in our book, *The Searchers*, now we wanted to broaden the subject matter. We still wanted to use the lens of the specifics of Genazzano, but would include in its scope a more universal message. This would be linked to the big themes of the U.N. seminar and Lisa's Findhorn experience, as well as the changes we observed in the village. By the time you left Wisconsin, we were both excited. This second book would revise *The Searchers*, and might be entitled: *The Wisdom of the Village in an Age of Scarcity: For Each Person a Piece of Land*.

Looking back, it's hard to believe that we didn't work on this new project until 25 years later. My job at the university was heavy duty, and after Lisa returned from Findhorn in latter 1976, we were very busy organizing the High Wind community. In effect, I had two fulltime jobs. Our family did take several short trips to Italy in the succeeding years, and we visited you at least once, but only for a few hours. Of course we continued to correspond, expanding on our book plans. I promised I'd be back in the village soon after retiring from the university at the end of the 1990s. You kept pushing, but I kept finding excuses.

One day in late 2000 Lisa and I got together with Karl Meyer, a family friend who edited the *World Policy Journal*. Karl had read *The Searchers*, published more than three decades previously. He was very curious about what was going on now in Genazzano, once Italy's most communist voting village. The USSR no longer existed and world communism had only a fraction of its previous influence. He commissioned me to contact you again and he'd publish the article we'd write.

Naturally, I couldn't wait to see you and check out Genazzano again. Lisa and I flew over in May 2001. You were 70 at that point, and I a bit older. We still had energy to tramp out into the fields to look up the small farmers. Some of the folks we'd spent hours with years before were still around, while others had died. We buckled down for a week, working dawn to dusk. Since the San Pio monastery was closed, Lisa and I found a room in the town's one new, small hotel. She's a painter as well as a writer, and she spent some of her time sketching village scenes, along with transcribing our interviews.

That week was very productive. We outlined the chapters of our new book. While we had both put on some years, we impressed ourselves with our burst of energy, not that different from our vigorous research of the early 1960s.

Your father had recently died and you wanted to share your deep emotion about that. You described his return from the war, World War I, with a crutch under his arm—the first wounded soldier from Genazzano.

A large crowd was waiting in the little station. There was not a window in the *vicolo* or *piazzetta* that didn't have people waving to the young man, the "*bel bersagliere*" as he was called. Once home, still in pain and discouraged, his wife consoled him and helped to reconstruct his desire to live. One day he got up from his bed with something of his old vigor. He began to believe that there was still a place for him. He'd been guaranteed a clerical job in a ministry, but he angrily declared that he would not finish his life behind a squalid desk as some bureaucrat. He was still a mason, a talented artisan, despite his handicap. When he was 15 he had learned to climb the tall ladder, and now he had to learn again with a peg leg. He had strong words for the *artigiani* who were beginning to leave their profession to take up easier employment. There was not a house in the village that his hand had not touched. Perhaps his best accomplishment was the impeccable restoration of the face of the San Pio monastery. He said, "I don't work just to get paid. The *artigiano* is an artist and has other values as well—the joy of a job well done."

One of our first stops was to Tramonta, the last of the old landed aristocratic class still around. After these many years, he remembered me. We drove up the half-mile driveway to his villa, now very rundown, his barn closed up. Chickens and ducks and rabbits ran around in the yard, but there was one nice vineyard in view. He was still a large man, though now old and somewhat bent. He had lost some teeth and had difficulty talking. We sat outside under a couple of large trees. We found a broken folding chair and two wooden chairs in a nearby shed, and a little table for beer. The last time we met he had offered us elegant wine.

Agriculture today is a disaster! You can no longer find anyone who wants to work. Our governors, who understand nothing, have completely neglected *la compagna* (the land). They've only developed industry, luring everyone into the big cities. Now even the well-to-do are abandoning their properties. Only later some of those people do return, by automobile, appearing as *signori*. I had two large olive groves—*bellissimi*— the best in the region. Today they're abandoned, they have become part of the woods because there are no workers. The *braccianti* (day laborers), register for unemployment assistance and exploit the state. Two years ago before I definitively decided to abandon the olives, I struggled to bring back the largest, most beautiful grove. I arrived at the employment office to request 20 men. Eleven showed up, I gave them wine, but they lasted only four days and some never lifted a hoe.

I will not need to suffer this much longer. My children, all seven of them, are *sistemati* (settled). Not one has remained in agriculture, which is *vergogna*, a shameful disaster. You know why all this has happened? It's the constitutional cowardice of our governors. They have ceded everything to the workers. They don't even respect the constitution they created. The worst Italians are the ones who are elevated to power. We need a strong government, one with a pulse, which actually stands for something. Everyone talks and criticizes, but they do nothing. The men of the Right who might have the competence and moral force are not even allowed to open their mouths. Fascism gave us a brief period of splendor, and now everyone is afraid of the communists. I do not see any salvation. I don't worry for myself as my life is about finished. I've taken care of all my family and grandchildren. The line of descendants is assured.

Genazzano is pathetic. Those in charge in the town here are the inept. They're only good for propaganda. They know and respect me, and won't touch me. People like myself, who understand the greatness of Italy, who do not forget but revere the past— now we are the few. It isn't that I want to play the hero; I only say what has been and what is true. I was clear with my children that I would remain on my land, but I told them not to stay because it is going nowhere. I made them all study; almost all of them have college degrees. They have the mentality of the best of the past, not that of these *moderni*. Now they must face a new future.

At the beginning of the 20th century there were four families of the old landed class, the so-called aristocrats. They held the old civilization in place following the Colonnas, who had ruled their feudal fiefdom for centuries. In the early 19th century the new bourgeois-professional classes emerged, but there were these families like Tramonta who still held the land and some remnants of the old power. After the 20-year fascist interlude, World War II brought democracy, and, as it's said, the revolt of the masses. For us Americans, observing this "changing of the guard" was fascinating, something outside of our own experience. While you, Athos, couldn't wait for this transition to run its course, I relished our contact with Tramonta, and also Patriottini. When these two men leave the scene, as they themselves told us, "No one will know what the old days were like."

Patriottini's life was bound up in one man: Benito Mussolini. Whether in formal military dress or in civilian clothes, usually white and perfectly tailored, this one-time fascist hierarch still had the look of a *signore*. He was glad to see us again, to review old memories. At times, when he spoke, he became deeply moved. His villa was near the town's principal church, with grapes and flowers outside the front door. The house was full of mementos of his career and references to fascism's important men.

Since we had met him previously, although many years ago, he arranged for us to meet this time with a high national official of the M.S.I. (*Movimento Sociale Italiano*), the current Fascist

Party. This official immediately launched into his remarks with a strong, confident voice, clearly his custom. We asked him the difference between the old fascism of Mussolini's day and the Right of today. I said that in America many think, with or without reason, that the Right in Italy today is merely a rehash of the old fascism. He responded:

In your American two-party system there is little difference between the parties; it's simply a way to bring change within the same political process. Democracy in Italy is very different: there are two fundamentally distinct alternatives: Christian Democracy (the government party), or the opposition Left, led by the communists. They say if you want to oppose the government, this means communism. People discontented with both the government and communism might like to consider the Right, but they are afraid. There will be no new "March on Rome"! Yesterday the *carabinieri* (national police) stopped two 16-year-olds, and the government media headlined "a grave fascist threat." In their knapsacks they had two hunting knives. Such paranoia!

Many Italians, including government supporters, would vote Right, but they don't, partly because of the grip of the Church. The priests in Genazzano still have a strong hold among some. People ask me about the link between fascism and an authentic Right. We have no fascist totalitarianism today, with regulation and absolute control; there is only the State. We live in a democratic system, the State has developed organically and there is individual autonomy. We still believe in real leadership, though—not in a negative sense, but representing a new radical front. We reject the Marxist formula where history is only economic, a function of materialist objectives. We also reject the idea of a mass of individuals running around chaotically, with no purpose. We present another way.

Athos, you kept pushing me to visit again a third key figure of Genazzano's history, your brother Federico. We found him in Rome, working to restore an ancient building in one of the most picturesque parts of the city. It was in the center, where many small roads and alleys converged. He was giving orders to one of his masons. He showed us the 15th-century architecture that he, a master of the medieval, was contracted to renovate. "It's a work of the cosmos," he said, "I deliver a perfect new creation. I don't stop until it's perfect."

I knew he had been a major figure of the World War II period and had led the anti-fascist resistance in Genazzano. Now, still an idealistic communist committed to building a new Italy, what changes had taken place in the quarter century since we last talked. Here's how he summed it up:

Changes? We must start again from scratch! There no longer is any difference between communists and Christian Democrats. The bureaucrats have triumphed. They trampled over the honest people, the idealists, those who fought sincerely for radical change. When I was most active some years ago in the Party, I often asked: how is it possible that the mediocre ones always win control of the apparatus? The parties now are all the same. There's virtually no difference. We arrived at the "historic compromise." Anyone who doesn't approve—out. I could cite hundreds of names of people who went from fascism to communism, and now are Christian Democrats. It's the same story.

All the diagnoses of our problems will result in change only when we ourselves recognize the problems and decide to act. Society will never progress if we give up the privilege to renew things. The prophetic spirits appear in every epoch, but then the initial sacrifice and fervor disappear. Today an unskilled worker with the bus line, Stefer, makes more than a highly skilled mason or carpenter. He sits punching tickets while the mason goes up in the air and takes risks that are necessary to build a house. How can we explain the wealth of all the party bureaucrats—PCI, DC, PSDI, PSI— they are all the same. Our only hope is the youth. Where else can we place our faith?

Much as we valued our return visits to these three historic figures of Genazzano, you and I also were commissioned to write an article for *World Politics*. We decided we'd get a credible commentary on the contemporary scene from Margherita, the village's current mayor. Smart, attractive, 38 years old, she was finishing her sixth year in office. Since her office in the municipal building was undergoing repairs, we found her and her staff in the famous castle built centuries ago by the Colonna family. Here is a paragraph from her statement, which we used in our article published in fall 2001:

> I can explain to you the new politics we've had in Genazzano since the end of the Cold War. "Communism" is out, and "democracy" of the Left or Right is in. There are no longer communists and fascists; everyone is a "democrat." I believe communism as it once was is finished, but the ideas are still there, helping with problems. I'm opposed to the right-wing coalition of Berlusconi, who recently won overwhelmingly in the national election. I've worked hard to assimilate our 200 immigrants from Albania and Morocco. Agriculture was once the economic base here. But that's finished. The small artisans, once the heart of the village, can't compete with modern industry. The Church is lazy, of little help. The future of the town is tourism, and I'm restoring the castle and the San Pio monastery, our big draws. I've just been elected to the national Chamber of Deputies on the democratic Left and will soon be leaving here.

We found Margherita more open and enlightened than the previous long-time communist mayor. After these and other interviews, I cornered you for some isolated downtime to share your own thoughts. I knew that no one else in Genazzano had your capacity to integrate the past and the present, to comprehend the essence of the village culture, and to tie this local story into the larger contemporary world.

The editor of *World Politics* wanted to know how it was that the right wing politician, Livio Berlusconi, won. You explained:

At one time in Italy there was a rigid polarization between the centrist Christian Democratic-led bloc and the monolithic communist and Left Socialist Alliance. Everything was spelled out clearly: the hammer and sickle for the communists; the crossed shield for the Christian Democrats. Today it's almost impossible to memorize the acronyms of all the political parties. Out of this confusion emerged Berlusconi, labeled politically Right, but he calls himself simply a democrat. He promises to do for Italy what he's done for himself. He's Italy's richest man. He controls three of Italy's largest media networks. His fingers are in everything: cinema, publishing, sports, real estate. He understands that Italy needs solidarity, and he promised almost everything. Time will tell, but this is why he won. He is one of Italy's most unscrupulous liars, and people in the village don't trust him. By definition, he's a monster. Yet some people like his freshness, and his resistance to efforts from the Left to intimidate him.

Berlusconi attracted plenty of media attention at that time. As a big personality, he tried to dominate the government. Eventually he got into all sorts of trouble, including with the law, and was removed from office. Now in this age of Donald Trump, I find some surprising similarities.

Athos, after all of our meetings during that week together, what, in essence, did we learn? You said you concluded that we had found four "new radicals." I think your meaning of "radical" has fundamentally changed. When we first met in the early '60s, just after you left the Communist Party, your focus was the class struggle—rich versus poor, mobilization to eliminate la miseria. "Radicals" were committed to social justice, to be implemented through revolutionary action to overturn the forces holding the controlling oppressive system in place.

I sense that your "radical" today in 2001 is more concerned with values. While the old problem of injustice still persists, now you see it against the fast-paced modern world of high consumption, people glued to electronic devices with no time for deep relationships. You say this is destroying humanity. More than ever, you see the intrinsic values of the village culture dying, being suffocated by the modern age. Your new radicals are less characterized by left vs. right, poor versus rich, liberals versus conservatives.

Here's how I understand that you would characterize the situation now:
+   There are those of the old political Left who oppose the corruption and pettiness of big government and big bureaucracy, and the mediocrity and selfishness of those in control;
+   There are those of the old Right who see in mass culture and mass democracy the destruction of the individual and his dignity;
+   There are those who grew up on the land, then left for the glitter of the city and its economic abundance, who then woke up and became disillusioned with the superficiality and shallowness of urban life;

- There are those who withdrew from it all, from the petty machinations of contemporary culture, who invoke certain philosophical principles about the cosmos and the natural order and espouse a consciousness that challenges much that's called "modern."

You say that today's REAL radicals are those who have lived close to the earth, who value the old rural civilization, *La Civiltà Contadina*. They have a certain humility in the face of the larger forces they can't control, so they tend to be superstitious and cling to a faith in the mysterious unknown. They are the craftspeople, maybe masons or farmers, finding reward in perfection, which is beyond price. They honor the sanctity of family and blood relationships.

You now have concluded that your image of an ideal "civilization" is today relegated to history in Genazzano, as in villages throughout the world. Agriculture as you once knew it is finished, the land is abandoned. Only big farms survive. The same is true for the class of skilled craftsmen, masons like your father and brother. They have disappeared. Before, one person worked on a project from beginning to end; today it's all specialized, where each person is responsible for only a small piece. There is no longer time or desire to learn the skills, so the youth go to the city to join the general labor force.

Our last night with you was very special. Lisa and I joined you for dinner with your daughter Catia, and her family. We arrived at their villa on the village periphery. She worked in the *municipio*, assisting the mayor. Her husband, Gianmarco, was an engineer. He drove his Alfa Romeo to Rome on the *autostrada* every day, his cell phone in constant use. He said his computer was the lifeblood of his professional life. Everyone chuckled when you said to all of us around the table: "I am *senza macchina, senza cellular, senza computer*" (without car, without cell phone, without computer). And you added "*senza solde*" (without money).

I will never forget Gianmarco's comment to you: "Athos, you may be the last traditional man in Genazzano who truly understands and lives the old culture. But you are also a modern man, knowledgeable of the world, who understands the transformation that is taking place. More and more people are seeing you as a prophet."

Once I returned to America, you kept hounding me to set a date for publication of our nearly completed research that was to be a new book. You were eager, as was I, to strike fast while our energy was high. I kept apologizing for putting it off, week after week, given my jammed-up schedule, but always confirming that, as for you, this was High Priority for me.

Before I write this last page of my letter to you, Athos, I must make a huge admission to the reader. You, dear Athos, my close friend, colleague, and fellow author, died in December 2001, seven months after we were last together in Genazzano. It is rare that I write a letter to a dead person. Although you died 16 years before I began this letter, I decided to write to you now because for me you are still in my living world. I still feel we are communicating. Of course, as is obvious, we never published the second book because you had left the scene, and I did not have the heart to continue it alone.

Luca Ciprotti, close to both of us, and the custodian of the San Pio monastery, sent me this email (one of the few people in the village on the Internet):

Caro Bel,

Athos left us the evening of 19 December, 2001, after three days of severe illness caused by his diabetes. He had suffered from diabetes for years, but he always seemed to overcome any problems. When he went into the hospital, he seemed on the mend, but his wife's sister told me there was probably a sudden abnormal reaction to insulin. Near the end, Athos insisted he wanted to return home, to pass his last moments in his familiar surroundings. He left us in the style and dignity that characterized his life.

The fatigue from his work with you when you returned to Genazzano in May this year did not cause this, since he had been working hard since then. He recently received a copy of the article you both wrote for the *World Politics Journal*, and he was very pleased. Two days before he died and was still lucid, he called me to be sure to advise you that your writing projects together prove that love and brotherhood can triumph in our human world.

Along with saying hello to you, I want to tell you I understand your pain of losing a friendship that lasted such a long time. Our village will profoundly miss a person like Athos, the only one who could understand the importance of values and traditions, which today have been taken over by the illusions of a materialistic world. I send affectionate greetings. Luca.

Reuben Harpole bridges
inner city and white establishment

Dear Reuben,

One day in the winter of 1964 you showed up at my home in Milwaukee's East Side. You said Dr. Kirk Petshek, professor of Urban Studies at the University of Wisconsin-Milwaukee, had sent you. You got right to the point, so as not to waste your time or mine. It turned out that we sat for two hours on the couch in my front room in animated discussion. Afterward, I checked out that you were a significant leader in the inner city who knew everyone there and that you were a man of action. You also were the advertising manager of the *Milwaukee Star*, Wisconsin's main black newspaper.

I had only joined the UWM faculty a year and half before, in August 1962, and most of my time had been engaged in international teaching and related projects. You were the first person from the African-American community I had met for any in-depth exchange. Recently my dean had asked me to participate in an ongoing informal seminar Petshek had organized with a handful of faculty. We were to begin to think through how the university could get more involved with the urban crisis that was escalating all around us. Joe Klotsche, the university provost, soon to be appointed chancellor, had started speaking out, saying that UWM, the campus located in the state's largest city, definitely had an urban mission. But no one knew what that was.

Before arriving in Milwaukee, I'd been working in Italy for many years, much of the time engaged in grassroots community organizing with homeless war victims, and then with refugees incarcerated for years in camps. The goal there was to design creative solutions that could offer new lives and hope for these disparate groups. Apparently my dean, and also Petshek, now thought that I could be one of the readily available assets in the university to figure out, in association with others, how to rebuild the lives of these also desperate people in Milwaukee's inner city.

Some folks in the university knew that after finishing my Ph.D. at the University of Chicago I'd been about to take a job with the U.S. foreign aid program in Northeast Brazil. A new initiative, the Alliance for Progress, was being organized to help produce positive change in one of the poorest, most underdeveloped regions of South America. This area was restive and believed to be ready for revolutionary violence. Senator Hubert Humphrey, who had followed my efforts with Don Murray to resettle refugees in Sardinia, had pushed for me to enlist in this Brazil endeavor.

At the last minute, the University of Wisconsin had recruited me. Given my Brazil interest, it then arranged that my first assignment was to attend an international conference in Rio de Janeiro and to lay groundwork for a research project in the Northeast of the country. Since the university's newly formed Land Tenure Center had just received a sizable government grant, that group encouraged me to design a proposal for Northeast Brazil. After several favorable hearings, I was contracted to organize a small team to fly there in summer 1963. I'd organize the groundwork for a project that subsequently could broaden into a major initiative. As one of the Center's earliest projects, it could pave the way for diverse efforts. Although my summer program went well and won strong support in Brazil, it quickly got mired at home in nasty university politics regarding ultimate control of the money. The university was forced to cancel the whole effort. As the project director, I ended up in limbo and my job itself was threatened. This helped to explain why my dean had pressed me to utilize my experience for new urban involvement needing urgent attention.

You, Reuben, of course knew none of this. Your interest was simply to find immediate help in a community that was ready to explode. You were in your early thirties, you'd lived all your life in Milwaukee and had held leadership roles in a range of community initiatives focused on the inner city. Former mayor Frank Zeidler had commissioned you to go to the university to seek more help. Your wife, Mildred, a very respected attorney, was heavily engaged in educational efforts, and was therefore an added asset.

While your interests were broad, you told me that your immediate attention concerned your chairmanship of the Community Relations Committee of the St. Elizabeth parish, located in the heart of the inner city. Due to urban renewal, there had been a tremendous influx of lower income blacks into the area and crime was rising. The excellent community school at St. Elizabeth's was desperate for help.

You also quickly summarized the larger picture. Housing conditions were some of the worst in the city. There was only one black principal in the city's whole school system, only one black alderman on the city council, no black judges. There was big demand for skilled labor, but blacks were excluded from the trade unions. Unrest was mounting, which in a couple of years led to widespread violence in Milwaukee and many cities. Apathy was becoming a way of life and there were few examples of success to inspire young blacks to finish their education.

As you continued, I was aware that you were an authentic observer who knew every block in the area and could define every need. I was impressed with your idealism. There was nothing in this for you personally. Your total focus was the community.

I promised to do what I could and was quite sure there'd be university interest. At the moment, though, my plate was full; soon I'd be off to Italy to gather data for a book I was committed to write. I'd get in touch in September on returning, having no idea what I was getting into.

I did call you in September. While I had a book to write, and still had some Brazil-related activities on my plate, I'd also been learning more details about urban needs through participation in Petshek's seminar. There were readings, speakers, discussions. Your approach was different; you wanted to introduce me to the *real* city. Now, for several months in every spare moment I could find, we prowled together around every corner of Milwaukee's poorest and most deteriorated neighborhoods. This was the so-called "inner core." We talked to ministers and teachers, visited shopkeepers, sat in bars, and met youngsters with their parents.

You introduced me to the movers and shakers of community organizations, political and civic leaders, and people who advocated strong measures to confront serious needs. While I felt Milwaukee's poverty in no way compared with the caves and ruins of Naples, or the *favelas* of Northeast Brazil, the people were certainly in desperate straits, and the university had a role to play.

Above all, this American urban crisis had its own special dimension—race. Milwaukee's inner core—several square miles directly north of downtown—was highly segregated. This was one of America's most racially ghettoized cities. Every economic, social, political, and educational factor common to disadvantaged central cities could be found here. Some of the minority population had moved to the periphery, the more affluent blacks migrated into the suburbs, but most remained.

The racism really hit home for me when we'd talk in your parked car in front of my house in Milwaukee's East Side and the police would stop by to inquire what you were up to in my neighborhood. A few months later when we attended a conference together in Atlanta, I reserved a hotel room for the two of us but was informed that this would be impossible. We had to arrange something with the hotel manager to get the room. Subsequently we entered the hotel bar for a sandwich and they told us that you were required to wear a necktie (but not me).

You knew Milwaukee's better neighborhoods intimately, and also the most depressed, violent places such as Hell's Corner where you risked your life just walking around. You understood the hostility that blacks felt toward authority, the pent-up anger. Your efforts at every turn were to try to build bridges between the races and classes, and to draw in the power structure, not an easy challenge. As we spent more and more time together I could see that your heart was full of compassion and you were a genuine man of peace, yet you also knew that sometimes militancy was the only way. As the months went by and we were seen together in public places, we sort of became known as the Bobbsey Twins. We had special roles: you were the front guy out in the community, and I was the key to get things to happen in the university.

As a starter, you brought together an informal group of concerned people from the St. Elizabeth parish, I drew in some folks from the Lay Life Committee of Plymouth Church that I attended, and you also invited several leaders of the Thirteenth Ward Council chaired by former Mayor Zeidler, including its amazing community networker, Una Colin.

We decided that a critical need was to learn what was going on with the youth in the inner core. Our planning group organized a house-to-house survey, talking to the parent or guardian in all the households that had young people aged 12 to 22. We enlisted Jonathan Slesinger, UWM's social survey research expert, who recruited 13 graduate students to work with us to design a comprehensive interview schedule. He identified a random sample of 60 blocks in the inner city. We trained 30 volunteers who lived in the area to work with us in completing 300 one-hour interviews in spring 1965. Apart from obtaining valuable data, we formed a cadre of skilled people who worked with us later, some of whom were hired as professional interviewers.

In the survey one very significant need kept surfacing: terribly deficient reading skills. Once a kid fell behind a couple of grades in reading, by the time he or she reached junior high school, everything else seemed to go wrong: lower academic achievement generally, higher absenteeism and tardiness, and behavioral/social problems of all kinds.

Our planning group, along with a cluster of parents, sponsored a summer demonstration reading project. Since we had begun working with the Robert Fulton Junior High School right smack in the middle of the area, we identified 42 students and the assistant principal to run the project, with assistance also from the UWM Reading Clinic. With four teachers, we also hired part-time, six residents who had helped in the survey. We called them community representatives, and they were to play crucial roles with us in the future.

As most of these kids had never taken learning seriously, every morning the community reps and others of us drove to their homes and literally kicked them out of bed. After class each day the entire group walked from their classroom provided by the university to the nearby Natural History Museum (where they had never been) for lunch provided by a local businessman.

Attendance for the seven weeks was almost perfect. At the final Recognition Night held at the UWM Student Union, attendance from the neighborhood was surprisingly high despite a violent rainstorm. A student with one of the lowest scores at the beginning read excerpts from essays written by the class. A girl from an extremely disadvantaged background sobbed when receiving her award.

Although this was not a large project, we recognized several positive benefits. Our inter-racial group, encompassing the larger Milwaukee community, was able to quickly mobilize resources and make things happen. Even a small project like this that was very well organized could generate its own rippling effects. And when a professional staff worked together with enthusiastic community people, a dynamic synergy was the result.

We learned from the 60-block survey that many inner core students graduating from high school were college material, but they had no idea how to process an application, get financing, and acquire essential language skills. We organized a summer pre-college English class at UWM, and you used your contacts with Milwaukee's Sears Roebuck store to organize "Personal Improvement" courses (also called "charm schools"). These became very popular; the first class graduated 80 girls.

We found our "ace in the hole" to be the community representatives. In the summer reading project they were the ones who won the support of both the young people and their families. When a kid wanted to give up, or a parent was too alienated to offer any enthusiasm, it was they who made the difference. Now, you and I sat down with the administration at Fulton Junior High School and we all designed a demonstration project that was able to build real communication between the school and its student families.

For the summer of 1966 we selected 15 teachers, each assigned 10 families with children at Fulton. Half of each week (20 hours) they committed to win the confidence of the students and parent(s) through whatever kind of fieldwork program they designed, carried out in the afternoons and/or weekends. The other half-week was for UWM classes and a weekly seminar to assess progress and planning innovation. The fieldwork goal was to convince the students that the teachers were not arrogant or condescending but interested in helping each person realize the full potential of his/her abilities. They could play games, go to the lake, go fishing, take in museums—whatever was needed to build rapport.

The key that made it work was 14 residents who made contact with the families. These families, in turn, found others on each block they then designated as block workers. This full community support made the project a huge success.

The project required full official cooperation of the public school central administration and school board. Since at this time there was high tension between the school system—considered narrow-minded and unresponsive—and the angry inner city community, you and I invited our friend Al Trostel, who belonged to one of Milwaukee's oldest, most prominent business families, to set up a lunch with Harold Story. You remember that Story was the most conservative, influential (and some considered most racist) school board member. At first he refused to meet, but Al convinced him. It took a while to break the ice, and then Story asked: What do you want from me? We told him we needed authorization and funding for our project. Story came through big-time and became one of our strongest allies.

You remember what happened next. Evaluation of the Fulton School pilot project, involving 15 teachers and 150 families, was so productive in cultivating a positive school culture that there was demand for a much larger initiative. The program expanded six-fold the next year, with 94 teachers, 900 families and 18 community representatives. Then in the third year it expanded citywide, to 200 teachers, 1,500 families, and 40 community representatives. By now the project's influence on the system had exercised an institutional impact, and it generated national publicity. You remember that Harold Story was a central actor; he obtained the school board authorization and the federal funding. Periodically, in order to assess progress, he invited us to his office for lunch and his famous chicken sandwiches.

One of the biggest discoveries from our work was the acknowledged huge breakdown of communication between the inner city community and those in power. The same problems we had found in the school-community relationship pervaded much of society: the police, the political and bureaucratic authorities, and definitely the corporate world. The same alienation, bitterness and anger that we found in the minority community was also present in the low-income white community.

This breakdown in the broader culture that we were beginning to comprehend and probe in the inner city community was becoming a national issue. Years later, writers such as conservative scholar Charles Murray, analyzed American culture in his book, *Coming Apart: The State of White America, 1960-2010*. He discussed this same chasm between the more powerful and powerless communities. It was not surprising that the same dynamic was very real and visible in the 2016 presidential campaign and led to the unexpected election of Donald Trump as president.

I don't need to remind you, Reuben, that by now our telephones were ringing off the hook. Individuals and agencies clamored for our advice. You were bubbling with pent-up ideas for projects. Once the word surfaced that there was someone at the university who really cared to cooperate with community leaders, ideas and proposals began pouring out of the woodwork. Our UWM dean, Fred Olson, mentioned to me on the way back from a meeting that the activities we were engaged in were the most significant efforts of the university in dealing with urban problems in the region.

While our work was going gangbusters, I must mention a not insignificant detail of my personal life. I was beginning to face serious domestic problems. Maybe this affected your home life too. I paid a price for being out almost every night for meetings and often on weekends. Your wife, Mildred, perhaps had worked out a routine with you. Like you, she was very sensitive to the stark community needs you'd been addressing for years. Presumably you had found your own ways to adapt. In our situation, Lisa and I had recently returned from working overseas. Even though the needs we had faced were dire, we worked together on projects and we also had help to take care of some family needs. Now in Milwaukee, Lisa considered herself "an indentured suburban housewife," responsible for all the household chores, raising two little kids, and supporting me in my profession, while she had little possibility for equally stimulating outlets. I was "out"— away from home and family much more than when we had lived abroad and shared all the exciting adventures and dreams. For a time, strains surfaced in our marriage.

Returning to our work together, our dean, Glen Pulver of UW-Extension, now pushed to establish a new department, the Center for Community Leadership Development (CCLD). Its focus: to creatively confront inner city poverty and racism. After a national search I was appointed chairman, and continued in this position for 22 years. You were the first professional staff from the black community to join University Extension in Milwaukee, and you continued with me for many years until we both retired.

The Wisconsin state government (Department of Industry, Labor and Human Relations), came to us saying that existing efforts to employ minorities in decent paying jobs had become a disaster. We established a "Sensitivity Committee" with executives of leading companies to develop a cadre of trainers. Their role: to work with management "to increase sensitivity to the life reality, expectations and behavior of the company's workforce." Our 30-hour training seminars included fieldwork and family visits, with assistance from our community representatives. You worked closely with the Milwaukee Voluntary Equal Employment Opportunity Council (MVEEOC) to recruit company members.

City and suburban churches were contacting us to design sensitivity programs for their congregations. This series ended up as the "Urban Training Program with Local Congregations." Purpose: to develop a process with church lay people to find meaningful solutions to the complex of problems of poverty, racial prejudice and discrimination. This effort expanded to two of Milwaukee's largest retail companies, Boston Store and Gimbels. The U.S. Department of Housing and Urban Development (HUD) and the Labor Department wanted in on the action for their staffs.

I can't forget our friend, Al Trostel, coming to you with a personal need. His family's company, the Trostel Tannery, faced potentially explosive issues with workers in the tannery's beam house, the factory's site where animal skins were separated from the flesh. The work required strong laborers, who happened to be all black, immersed in excruciating conditions of heat and foul odors.

Here seminar-type programs were useless. This was a high-stress, face-to-face situation with counseling needed to relieve the tension and seek long-term solutions. You played a critical role.

In this period you were all over the map, so full of ideas and projects that you made everyone's head spin, mine included. One series of initiatives I'll mention because it produced amazing results with inner city youth. Called Summer Prep, the format was to harness the talents of some of the best private high schools in Wisconsin. They happened to be associated with the Catholic Church for the benefit of disadvantaged inner city youth. PREP meant a Program of Recreation and Educational Preparation.

We've previously mentioned that our research confirmed that the middle school-age years—the three years before high school—were critical in determining the academic and career future of kids, most especially those who were "marginal" and could go either way in terms of moving forward or getting dragged down with multiple problems. You contacted the administrators and the most creative teachers at such high-achieving schools as Marquette University High School, Divine Savior High School, Francis Jordan High School, and Campion High School located in southwestern Wisconsin. Using small contributions from local foundations, we developed proposals with each school to sponsor summer programs that combined academics (e.g. language, reading, mathematics), recreation (e.g. team sports, drama, art, music), and leadership development (e.g. group planning, taking responsibility, role playing, and exchanging ideas). You identified the students who would participate, and you often contacted parents to get them involved, including for graduation celebrations. You inspired the schools to use some of their most resourceful staff.

The Campion School was specially challenging. As a residential school, the students had to leave home. Often they were known troublemakers, including gang leaders. Like all participating students, most were black, while most school staff were white. Apart from all the usual academic and behavioral issues, there were race-related controversies. One time when the whole project was about to blow up, we designed with the Campion staff a "genius model"—to put the kids, including gang leaders, in charge of making and enforcing the rules. Some excelled with their new responsibilities, and years later we heard that this experience was central to personal success.

In 1976 a United States District Court handed down a historic decision: to desegregate. It declared that the Milwaukee public schools "have knowingly carried out a systematic program of segregation affecting all the city's students, teachers and school facilities and have intentionally brought about a dual school system." This brought Milwaukee into the long-smoldering national struggle that arose in 1954 when the U.S. Supreme Court case, Brown vs. Board of Education of Topeka, declared that "separate but equal" had no place in public education. You and I and our other colleagues were all too familiar with the issues being addressed: poor inner city school performance, racial segregation in housing that had concentrated the lower income black community in the inner city, and racism scattered throughout governance structures and in the corporate world. While we had implemented an array of worthwhile school programs on a smaller scale, the city of Milwaukee was now being forced by law to act.

The first issue was to prevent violence. The MPS Board was dead against the ruling to desegregate and ran up a huge legal bill in a futile effort to appeal it. Residential and school segregation in Milwaukee was well known. Enrollment at 73 MPS buildings was more than 90 percent white, while in 31 buildings it was more than 90 percent black. This was a dual school system in which blacks received a second-class education. In their struggle to integrate, would Milwaukee end up like Boston and Louisville, with riots and bloodshed? You remember that our university department worked closely with the churches and many civic groups. Milwaukee ended up as a national model for peaceful integration.

The court-imposed integration initiative also offered a huge opportunity to rethink the schools, to promote quality education along with integration. Here was a once-in-a-lifetime chance! Unhappily, the prevailing integration assumption was that by mixing up the races simply through busing, automatically this would improve quality without other specifically designed actions. This conclusion was drawn from prevailing research, specifically the much-publicized recent study, *Equality of Educational Opportunity*, chaired by Johns Hopkins sociologist James Coleman.

We offered the school board an excellent model of what could be done that combined integration with improving quality. This was at Riverside High School on Milwaukee's East Side, which our own son Eric, was now attending. Violence had broken out between black and white students about who would be chosen prom king and queen. While a small event, it threatened to become huge. The school administration at Riverside had difficulty not just with this matter, but with the large pressing issues of race and quality brought on by the court decision. We pulled together parents and teachers in community meetings to offer a proposal: Let's not deal with just the prom violence: Let's think about designing first-rate education here.

Called the Riverside Educational Improvement Project (REIP), we organized task forces probing everything from long-term demographic trends to state-of-the-art ideas about each academic subject. We viewed the high school and its seven feeder elementary schools as one interdependent cluster to function as a whole. What was happening in the lower grades obviously had massive impact later. We attracted enthusiastic community involvement; 100 parents were drawn in and they did their homework. The project became known citywide because what we were doing voluntarily to maintain racial balance in one small area, the court order was forcing the city to do. Michael Kirkhorn, education writer with the *Milwaukee Journal*, wrote: "This is the best thought-out proposal we've seen anywhere, concentrated in a single school district."

The school board and the integration officials lauded our proposal. Then they did just the opposite. They focused only on racial numbers, assuming quality would result. This was a transportation strategy, not a quality strategy. Most parents wanted minimum busing and keeping neighborhood schools, which was our plan. But the official strategy maximized busing and tore up neighborhoods. School system statistics showed that about 85 percent of the students who were bused were black. Students from one elementary school population might be bused to 26 different schools as part of the integration numbers game. In the case of our Riverside model, the cluster idea and high-quality learning plan were made NOT to function, although our proposal did get some funding (especially for a new gym).

Most of us, from community activists and academics to parents, supported the concept of racial integration and thus were reluctant to criticize what was happening. But in conferences and workshops we spelled out what would inevitably occur nationally as had happened in Milwaukee. Those who could afford quality schools—which included many of our Riverside parents—left town for the suburbs and exurbs. Or they transferred from public to private schools, including charters. The lower income population, which in heavy numbers was black and Hispanic, remained in the central city. The public schools once again became minority schools. With higher needs and lesser resources for education, quality was the loser. Today most big city public schools remain heavily minority and too often lower quality. With many others, we know that a huge opportunity was lost!

We were tapping into a very sore spot in the larger culture. From the first days when you and I began working together, our own relationship gradually evolved. We forgot we were a white man and a black man. As our staff expanded both in numbers and inter-racially/inter-ethnically, we became a little community. Although we had varied backgrounds, we shared values. We also knew in the school integration struggle that much of the challenge had to do not with race but *class*, although there tended to be a close correlation between race and poverty in the inner city.

Indelibly impressed in our minds was President Lyndon Johnson's *Report of the National Advisory Commission on Civil Disorders of 1967*:

> Our nation is moving toward two societies, one black, one white—separate and unequal. . . . Discrimination and segregation have long permeated much of American life. They now threaten the future of every American. . . . To ensure our present course will involve the continuing polarization of the American community, and ultimately the destruction of basic American values. The alternative is not blind repression or capitulation to lawlessness. It is the realization of common opportunities for all with a single society.

You remember when Dean Pulver sat down with us and said: "We ourselves have great experience with this subject. Milwaukee is one of America's most racist cities. Let's craft a proposal for the Ford Foundation and demonstrate to the country what is possible." In my own case, I had just been in Albany, N.Y., speaking at a workshop organized by the state government on how universities could play a role in dealing with the country's urban and racism problems. After hearing my discussion, they urged that we in Wisconsin design a national program.

Pulver convinced us that what we came up with was excellent: a 21-page request for $773,000 over three years for "Development of a Regional Training and Action Center to Confront the Problems of Institutional Racism." We noted the positive evaluations of everyone we'd worked with and called for a creative partnership between government and local communities. Using our experience in preparing local leaders, we'd organize a core of trainers to implement operational programs with governmental agencies, business and industry, religious organizations, educational institutions, and the general public. The program would be based in our university department. It would use the full resources of the University of Wisconsin and develop a model and training materials that later could be applied nationally.

You and I and Dean Pulver met with the Ford and Carnegie Foundations in New York. They were excited with our proposal and told us the country should listen to us, but they didn't give us any money. I was not altogether unhappy with this result. Important as the proposal's goals were, this could be an all-consuming undertaking, while at this time our work was already spreading in many directions.

Before we left New York the three of us sat together in one of our hotel rooms reviewing what had happened. We were not despondent that the foundation bureaucrats rejected our proposal. But we were crystal clear as to why most efforts dealing with the inner city complex of problems brought less than maximum benefits. The failure stemmed from the faulty way we defined the problems and organized to deal with them. This included our proposal. Take these two foundations. We had met smart, well-intentioned people. Each foundation was full of offices with "experts" whose names on their doors identified the tiny slice of an inner city problem each one was responsible for.

But the pathology of the inner city was a composite of many causes—systems of problems. The foundations needed some wise holistic thinkers who could figure out how to pull together all these isolated fragments, these individual names on the doors, into real-world wholes. Admittedly, this was hard to do. It was ludicrous to think that school desegregation and better schools would happen simply by moving around bunches of students, given the multiple variables to be accounted for.

Take the "reading problem," such an important component for dealing with inner city school age youth. A package of factors had to be recognized, including the following:

+ **The School System:** ability of the teachers and administrators to reach the child; relevance of the school curricula to the child's background; school-community relations
+ **The Home Environment:** parental support; presence of an adult to assist the child with studying; attention to family health and nutrition; sanitation; heat; study area without distraction
+ **The Economic System:** family employment; necessity of the child to go out to work at early age; opportunity or ability to buy books and supplies
+ **The Political System:** family acceptance of legitimacy of school authority; participation in school decision-making

Had the school system, with the ample resources at its disposal to implement desegregation, marshaled the best experience and brains to make this kind of analysis, today's public schools would likely be very different.

Remember that at one of our staff meetings this nagging question showed up. Notwithstanding all of our worthwhile projects, we agreed that "a lot is going on but a lot more could be happening." This meant that we were loaded with activities but were we getting to the fundamental causes of the problems? Take my experience in Naples. We were distributing food, clothing and medical care to the homeless living in the caves—valuable day by day to keep them alive—but we weren't attacking the root causes: finding jobs and housing and preparing the people to leave the caves. Finally, with Casa Mia's focus on education and dealing with whole families, and cultivating social conscience in the larger community along with the relief operation, we achieved far more.

Reuben, you brought up again the St. Elizabeth Community School. Its board president had asked you to help save the school. The Catholic Archdiocese had been subsidizing a number of inner city schools, but the financial crunch forced it to cut funds. Local leaders responded by creating seven community schools, yet they, too, were now threatened with closure. The best one was the Harambee School in the St. Elizabeth parish. This was the same area where you and I began. We met with the school board and told them: If this is really a *community* school, you the community must be empowered to make it work. If there's strong community commitment, we'll help.

This led to the founding of the Harambee Revitalization Project (HRP). *Harambee* was Swahili for "Let's Pull Together." You know the story well: many meetings were arranged with the school leaders and others in the surrounding area. The result was a design for a comprehensive development plan to advance the wellbeing of people in a 12-square-block area around the school. We locked in federal funding through Title 1 of the Higher Education Act, which we renewed several times.

The first challenge was to find a handle for the starting point of this undertaking, which in time expanded to encompass 160 blocks with a population of 30,000. A policy committee was established with representatives from the Harambee School along with the contiguous neighborhood and several university departments and other educational institutions. At the outset you were project director. The policy group had good people. It hired a community planner who lasted for a year, and then two respected economic development consultants from the community who, after a year of study and numerous community meetings, produced a thick goals blueprint. I offered several urban politics classes that brought in city officials and corporate leaders as well as local people and regular students.

While all this activity brought much community participation, let's be candid; there were not many concrete results. You resigned as director but remained heavily involved. Community people were elected to the board. Pulver shared our frustration; this was one more well-meaning effort with some educational benefits but there wasn't much tangible progress toward the big goal of community revitalization.

Now we organized another university class, but this time with grassroots folks from the blocks who were hurting and complaining bitterly about poor city services. It was not held on campus but one night a week in the public library located in the heart of the area. I invited Alderman Ben Johnson to join me; he represented this jurisdiction on the city council. The first night several residents described emotionally one block with abandoned homes and overgrown grass full of rats and garbage and kids hanging out with drugs. The city obviously had no interest in cutting the grass and cleaning up. Ben and I asked what they'd done about it other than complain. The neighborhood folks had no idea. We discussed a basic concept of political science: input-output analysis. You take action specifying your needs and demanding response from those who hold power to do something about it. Ben explained in simple terms how to contact governmental officials and expect results.

Over the next weeks the class set up a steering committee of neighborhood people and a few professionals (e.g. the alderman, county supervisor, etc.). Class members from the community were each assigned one block, usually where they lived. Their target: to go house-to-house and get specific information on unmet needs that required outside help. They brought the data for class analysis and action. Their work was so successful that we called them block leaders. They learned a new word: *ombudsman*. This meant they would formulate the needs they'd uncovered in a way that they could bring the issues to the attention of elected officials and administrative agencies. They'd also take responsibility for following through to assure that actual delivery of a particular service happened, or to learn why not.

This class action program proved so successful that participants didn't want the class to end. This led to our creating the Harambee Ombudsman Project (HOP). We hired one of the most effective block leaders, Agnes Cobbs, to join our university staff as coordinator. Agnes was a charismatic, self-effacing civic leader with dynamic energy. She built up HOP in the next years to well over 200 block leaders. With ongoing training held at the library one night a week, and strong support from Alderman Johnson who became city council president, and Milwaukee County Supervisor Emil Stanislawski, the HOP became a model for the whole city and also got to be known nationally. I recruited a creative pre-law student, Todd Honeyager, who joined Agnes in coordinating the project in its early years.

We might add that Agnes had already distinguished herself in working with us to help coordinate 25 tutorial centers we organized, scattered around the inner city (along with Mary Suttle, another effective block leader we also brought in). We had contacted the ministers who allowed their church basements to be used. We enlisted volunteer tutors, half of them drawn roughly from the inner city and half from elsewhere, including the suburbs. The UWM Reading Clinic trained the tutors and evaluated their work. The schools greatly appreciated this contribution, although it did not resolve fundamental school problems of quality.

The HOP spurred the evolution of Harambee Revitalization Project efforts. With its impressive grassroots contacts and increasing public visibility, the HRP pushed into three new directions. In passing, it's worth mentioning that we built up my university department organically, person by person, along the way changing its name from CCLD (Center for Community Leadership Development) to CUCD (Center for Urban Community Development). Each staff member began as a volunteer. With exceptional skills they combined strong motivation with our mission of using university resources to confront inner city poverty and racism. You know, Reuben, that it started with you: at first you were financed with a small foundation grant until we arranged full university support. Next came Agnes and Mary.

Gene Thuot joined us from the corporate world. He combined a graduate degree in continuing education with recognized skills in construction and business practices. He first organized programs to assist community people to get into civil service and office employment (e.g. preparation to pass civil service tests for government jobs, and typing and accounting skills for businesses). Then, as the HOP stirred up homeowners and renters to upgrade their housing, often in disastrous condition, he worked with a cadre of community volunteers and various public agencies to create the Harambee Development Corporation (HDC) and the Home Maintenance Project. The group provided home repair services to Harambee residents and encouraged maintenance of the housing stock. A paint-up operation was established with donated materials. With considerable impact, he and HDC, along with the county housing director, carried out a study of inner city vacant lots, and recommended policy changes.

Another key person was Dan Folkman. As we began mounting community surveys with various community groups, we were in desperate need of help to process all the computerized data. With advice from my UWM political science colleagues, I recruited this bright grad student. Over time he, like all of us, expanded into many assignments. He and I also invested considerable energy in conceptualizing our work as a functioning example of the university role in urban problem solving. Our published case study in community-university participation, "A Reporting and Planning Model for Urban Community Development," was widely circulated.

Later on, when our department entered into the whole area of ecological planning and sustainable development, all of us played a variety of different roles. For example, the University of Wisconsin delegated to our department responsibility for implementing a sizable U.S. Department of Energy contract to make energy audits of inner city homes. Agnes, with HOP, identified needs and helped to harness community support. Gene trained and supervised the auditors. Dan developed pioneer eco-models for utilizing solar energy for home hot water systems. We worked with a variety of agencies in eco-planning, including Goals for Greater Milwaukee 2000. In later years the department took on major responsibility for planning and teaching a futures curriculum, as well as organizing national conferences to build a more sustainable world.

You took special interest in HRP's health committee, chaired by your wife Mildred. A television program graphically portrayed the horrific status of health in Milwaukee's black community. The nurse at the Harambee School told the HRP board her concern about the health of the families of attending children. The city health commissioner provided the health committee a neighborhood outreach worker to do initial screening. This pointed to the urgent need for a front-line neighborhood-based health program. It would not cater to expensive high-end services but would give residents health screening, preventive health care education, and an accessible community health clinic offering multiple services, all under one roof. The primary care would include everything from dental work to eye exams and fitting for glasses, to basic services and referrals for more specialized needs. It helped with insurance claims, waivers for the elderly, and counseling on infants and children for nutrition.

You recall the numerous meetings over several years when we rounded up all the key institutions and health leaders. It was a dizzying amount of dialoguing to explore what a community health center should look like. The result was dramatic: sizable funds were granted by the Robert Wood Johnson Foundation to create the multi-purpose Isaac Coggs Community Health Center (Isaac Coggs was a prominent local civic leader in the black community, now deceased, and husband of Marcia Coggs, former splendid block leader, later elected to the Wisconsin legislature).

Another big initiative happened with the advice of Virginia Parkman, a planner in the Milwaukee office of the Wisconsin Department of Health and Human Services and consultant to Harambee. You remember she was a personal friend of ours, always alerting us when the state was examining new approaches to human services delivery. Since we knew through HOP block work that one-third of Harambee area residents received some form of public assistance, and the providing bureaucracies were too often unresponsive and inefficient, here was a great opportunity for radical improvements. Alderman Johnson and Supervisor Stanislawski were eager to help. In short order, HRP's Task Force on Human Services designed an impressive proposal for "Creation of a Viable Community Service Center or the Delivery of Social Services in an Inner City Neighborhood."

This set in motion a string of events over the next several years, resulting in policy impacts not only for Harambee but for Milwaukee County. Stanislawki got the county to authorize and fund Harambee to develop a pilot plan. The process, chaired by Agnes Cobbs, joined community people with officials from the key agencies. The county executive also appointed a steering committee that included two representatives from UWM—the Social Work dean and me—to develop a countywide policy that would include the pilot work of Harambee. Dan Folkman chaired a comprehensive community survey on welfare needs, and I offered two UWM seminars on Human Service Delivery and the Political System. All of this produced ideas that fed into policy-making.

From the first days of our work with Harambee, our overall objective was to create a "Healthy Community." Then the question came up: What is a healthy community? Not just physical health, but all-around health and wellbeing. You remember, Reuben, we'd go to the blackboard and doodle with whatever far-out idea emerged. One afternoon you got me to chatter about my experiences years earlier to resettle refugees in Sardinia. That project goal was to create a model for a viable community of 15 refugee families—people who'd been cramped for years in barbed-wire camps, and who then went on to live healthy, "normal" lives.

In recalling this experience, I noted that the Italian Government's economic development agencies would commit to give us significant funding IF we'd draw up a *Piano di Massimo*—a Master Plan. They'd fund the whole plan but only by our describing each specific project: the houses we'd build, the land we'd irrigate, the electric power we'd bring in.

Building on this discussion, we moved to defining the "master plan idea" of what a healthy Harambee community would look like. The essential factors of community health we called "variables." For operational simplicity, we limited ourselves to four essential variables: economic health, educational health, environmental health and political health.

We recruited the most knowledgeable, creative minds we could find in the university to work with us and the community to figure out what each of these meant in describing a healthy community. Thus was born one of the more intellectually stimulating endeavors you and I and Dan worked on. We enlisted economist Gary Gappert from the Department of Urban Affairs, Marty Haberman from the School of Education, Bob Beckley from Architecture for environment, and political scientists Neal Riemer and Dan Folkman. Excited to participate, these colleagues formed teams of graduate students and Harambee residents. They came up with perceptive findings that we all discussed in seminars. Word filtered out that the National Institutes of Mental health (NIMH) in Washington was interested in us for their metropolitan problem-solving. They urged us to draw up a proposal for a sizable grant. Each of our team leaders agreed to commit up to one-third of their time for two years if we were funded. The goal: to design a model for national use.

Our university administrators were so excited with the cutting-edge package our teams developed for an inner city community health strategy that they were convinced we'd get funded. A high-powered evaluation group organized by NIMH spent two days with us in Milwaukee. They were impressed and indicated that eventual funding was likely, but no money could be given until we invested several more months to develop further our ideas for wide applicability. While we did receive several small grants, our busy faculty decided that they had no more time or energy for further proposal preparation. We continued to use our ideas with Harambee and other community groups.

One positive outcome emerged from our meetings with the Milwaukee and Chicago offices of the U.S. Department of Housing and Urban Development (HUD). HUD was very interested in our comprehensive planning efforts with Harambee, the Community Health initiative, and our various schemes to build interrelationships between the city and the suburbs. We participated in a conference in Minneapolis where a strategy was under development to interrelate an inner city neighborhood like Harambee with a contiguous suburban area. I wrote an article in the *Milwaukee Journal*: "Theory on 'New Towns' Pairs City Area, Suburb." It summarized forward-looking urban thinking drawn from Minneapolis and elsewhere. All of this dialogue on new communities spurred two new initiatives in our department.

While Dean Pulver was questioning the nebulous nature of the early planning with Harambee, he was enthusiastic about our utilizing the new communities legislation recently approved by Congress. HUD gave our department a planning grant to conceptualize how Harambee could link up with an outlying area, be it a nearby suburb or even the creation of a new town—a "paired town" strategy. We hired several bright graduate students, assisted by a couple of university faculty, to collaborate with Gene Thuot in developing a plan. We organized seminars with some of the most creative people in the city and county and from business. We talked to Wisconsin's most influential congressman, Henry Reuss, who was interested in a new town for Wisconsin. We compiled an inventory of 40 top decision-makers in companies in the Milwaukee metropolitan area to learn their intentions for the next five years. We utilized professor Grasskamp from the Madison campus, a wheelchair quadriplegic who was a genius running an international empire of urban developers.

Pulver was so turned on that he asked me to join him to meet Don Percy, vice-president of the UW System central administration. The goal: to seek major funding for an "objective, authoritative information center on the state of the art in new community building." This was still a virgin knowledge frontier; it would be located in our department but would draw in many resources. The center would pull together the multiple facets of our work and link with other university departments. The output could offer value for both the region and nationally. Since Percy wanted us to enlist other sectors of the university, we drafted a letter that the UW-Extension chancellor signed, addressed to the UWM academic deans to identify interested faculty. We conducted a survey, coordinated by Dan Folkman, and found 80 faculty members very interested in offering their talents to the potential center.

About this time Donovan Riley had been appointed assistant chancellor at UWM. The university directed him to take a new look at the university's urban mission and how the statewide UW-Extension and the UWM campus could work more closely. He and the two administrations established a Task Force on Urban Extension, with faculty from both sectors. Since as a joint appointment I was related to both, the Task Force asked that I develop a mission statement for creation of a new entity, the Division of Urban Outreach (DUO). We pulled together a nucleus of faculty that prepared a 27-page document for the Task Force.

Since Riley had personal contacts with budget decision-makers in the Wisconsin State Government, and they in turn were connected with counterparts in the federal government, he felt this was an ideal moment to design a comprehensive proposal seeking monies to enhance a University of Wisconsin national leadership role toward solving urban problems. We consulted with others in the university and community to document a series of innovative proposals: Urban Wisconsin Idea Decision Items. We expanded on the university's famous "Wisconsin Idea" philosophy—that the boundaries of the university's mission encompass the whole state as well as the individual campuses. This successful model had been critical in modernizing agriculture and enriching small towns, using state and federal monies. The challenge now: could this model also be implemented for urban problem solving? This was the key statement of our final document:

> The University of Wisconsin can pioneer in drawing substantial federal resources on a long-term basis to universities engaged in urban problem solving, and in structuring an apparatus whereby federal resources work together with those of state, city and county government for making full utilization of university resources for urban solutions.

These initiatives were also buttressed by a recent publication of the *Journal of Extension*. This was a quarterly journal of university programs with a national editorial committee. The *Journal* normally focused on the historical interest of extension programs in agricultural and rural development. I was asked to serve as guest editor for a special urban-related issue. It included a statement by the administrator of the Federal Extension Service, based in the U.S. Department of Agriculture on urban extension work. We contacted all the directors of university extension programs across the country. Most indicated that far more urban activity needed to be done.

Rightly or wrongly, in my own mind the times had brought us to a kind of peak moment. Riley and I, as well as you and our other associates, were beginning to imagine a vision of a new kind of university with innovative urban involvements and strategies. With these varied initiatives in different stages of development, it seemed there was an outside chance that this slow-moving institution could make a significant move forward.

Looking back now after half a century, this appeared to be one of those memorable possible turning points for breakthroughs. For you and me and our other colleagues, creativity was in the air. High-level support from the university was there. Funding streams seemed to be opening up. In our more skeptical reflections, we wondered: *Is all this energy going to take us anywhere?*

In these last years Pulver and other administrators were under relentless pressure to show "tangible results." In the past we'd heard this same refrain but now it was louder. Despite the positive, even exciting prospects of the initiatives underway, ominous trends were appearing. With Pulver, who of course was much closer to what was happening in university central administration and in the state legislature, we sensed that his positive expectations were dimmed by the big push of the authorities to trim budgets across the board. As a department chairman, I was getting notices that the university's "public service" mission was being changed by the call for every department to raise "significant program revenue." This meant emphasizing programs that generated income as well as solving problems. Our inner city efforts had concentrated on working with the lower income population, with few resources to pay for much of anything, and also on longer-term endeavors that took years to show meaningful results. This new focus on money and short-term results, therefore, had dramatic impact. In the view of many, by the end of the 1970s the "War on Poverty" and the threat of urban violence were history.

Now, looking at several years in capsule form, this is what happened. Pulver resigned as dean of Economic and Environmental Development and returned to teaching. Since his was one of the largest, most complex divisions of University Extension, and since he was by far the most innovative dean we'd ever had, his leaving had significant bearing. Two chancellors of University Extension who had been supportive of our department, also resigned in a several-year period. Percy left the university for a new job. Not long after, Donovan Riley resigned. A new Division of Urban Outreach was established, bringing together Extension and the UWM campus (I was elected first chairman of its faculty). But the larger designs we envisioned remained stillborn.

You too, Reuben, were rightly frustrated. As the cofounder of our department, which was mandated to deal with inner city poverty and racism, you now wrote me a terse letter: "Our department has now grown to the point where I think my contributions are no longer needed." You were reacting to criticism of the Harambee Project and the seeming downplaying by central administration of our hard-fought contributions to inner city betterment. You asked: What's more important for our tax dollars than to confront poverty and racism? I talked you out of resigning and we worked together for many more years, but our world was changing.

Many of our inner city projects continued and new emphases emerged. Our department branched out from a concentrated inner city focus. We helped establish two new innovative public schools, organized several national conferences on high priority issues, and I expanded my teaching to futures studies, contributed to major national initiatives toward building a sustainable world. (These are discussed in subsequent letters.)

With your ongoing amazing range of contacts, you continued to make yourself felt all over the city. You assisted the Helen Bader Foundation to utilize its resources in many creative projects. The Community Brainstorming Conference you organized convened top leaders each month to address salient civic issues of the larger community. I resigned as CUCD chairman in 1990, to be replaced by our very competent colleague, Dan Folkman. He served for a couple more decades, and then, in turn, was replaced by another worthy department member, Kalyani Rai.

With both of us now long since retired from the university, I look back and memorable thoughts come to mind about the adventures in which you and I and our associates participated:

- We helped the University of Wisconsin direct new resources to urgent needs related to inner city poverty and racism.
- We offered a kind of skeleton outline of key components for a comprehensive urban policy, which included: an approach to community analysis and revitalization and grass-roots contact as exemplified by the Harambee-related projects; an analytical framework for understanding Community Health;

multiple approaches to improve better schools, including focus on reading and radically improving school-community communication; and trained community volunteers as problem-solving ombudsmen with decision-makers.

+ We designed a typology for interrelating university educational functions (teaching, service, and experimentation) with anticipated kinds of projected change that focused on individuals, organizations, and policy formation—all in the framework of viewing community development as an incremental process directed toward strategic objectives and long-term goals.

+ We found ways to utilize diverse and often under-utilized university assets for urban problem-solving, which included redefining the meaning of "student," which brought formerly left-out lower income people into higher education, and tapping faculty skills for novel non-traditional endeavors.

Reuben, I decided to write this letter to you in particular, although we know our work involved a wide array of other dedicated associates. You were my first major introduction to immersion in the inner city and racism challenges. We faced recurring ups and downs—the world and the university changed around us. The regular paid staff in our university department, and countless other university colleagues, and hundreds, even thousands of people both in the inner city and larger community, all merit mention. But this is a short letter.

This communication to you would be incomplete without noting distinctive honors and awards you have received for your indispensable role both in the university and in the larger community. While the list is long, we include several: honorary doctoral degree of Humane Letters from UWM (2005); Frank Kirkpatrick Award of the Milwaukee Foundation; the Metropolitan Milwaukee Civic Alliance Community Service Award; the Vatican II award (with your wife Mildred); and the SBA Small Business Advocate of the Year Award.

Important as the awards are, there's something much more valuable to share. From the early years, we developed a relationship as idealists using whatever energy and talent we could muster to confront society's ills. While sometimes we were ivory tower, with our colleagues we did achieve results. We cared about each other's welfare and followed each other's families. When we began, your kids were infants and I watched as they matured; you did the same with mine. I was always interested in what Mildred was up to, and you followed Lisa's projects. When we dealt with difficult situations, such as when school board influential Harold Story was vilified as a racist, we understood, but we also cut through the outer cover to come to appreciate him on the human level. When certain folks criticized us for not joining Father Groppi and the militant Commandos to march, we respected their efforts as allies but our stance was to build bridges across chasms of hostility throughout the community. All of this was not a political or economic exercise but deeper work.

Much has happened since we and our partners began more than half a century ago. Inner cities were in turmoil, violence was rife, poverty was deep and accentuated by race.

Today, unhappily, these same problems persist. Were you and I and our colleagues starting out again, I'm sure the following three issues, among others, would be among those central to our mission.

- *The growing inequality of income and opportunity.* While our country's wealth has prospered as never before, the American dream of upward mobility and a far better life for many was more prevalent in the 1970s than it is today.
- *Chronic joblessness on the horizon.* Today's economy can produce all the goods and services our society needs without our total labor force. Modern technology and globalization have brought spectacular benefits and total wealth has increased dramatically. And even though many people today are employed, fewer people are likely to be needed for fulltime well-paying jobs.
- *Our education is falling behind many of the world's advanced nations.* The capacity to think creatively and willingness to share in problem-solving and building community are sorely needed as learning institutions confront today's priorities.

I can picture you, exactly as many decades ago, showing up and launching immediately into a no-nonsense exhortation: "Let's get to work!"

Brazilian academic Paulo Elpidio supports
American charged with espionage

Dear Paulo Elpidio,

You and I worked together in Fortaleza for only one year, 1967-68, but it was heavy-duty eventful. That's half a century ago, and our only subsequent contact has been mainly via the Internet—yet you have no idea what impact my experiences with you and Brazil have had on my life since then! The fact that my memories remain so vivid simply confirms that our adventures are unforgettable.

You may remember that I had worked in war-destroyed Italy for more than six years in the 1950s, including with the United Nations, and then I joined the University of Wisconsin in 1962. During the Italy period I met Senator Hubert Humphrey, a major American political leader (he ran for U.S. president in 1968). Humphrey was very interested in our work in community development and resettling refugees in depressed areas. On my return home in the early 1960s, he urged me to build on my experience with Latin cultures by joining the American government's new "Alliance for Progress" program in Northeast Brazil. I was nearly ready to accept a position, to be based in Recife, when at the last minute I accepted a professorship at the University of Wisconsin, moving to its Milwaukee campus (UWM).

In late 1961 the Northeast Brazil region was being discussed in Washington as the site for a massive "pilot project" for the Alliance for Progress. President Kennedy was asking for regular reports on the area. A stream of high-level officials visited the region, and President Goulart of Brazil was invited to the United States. An agreement was signed and money allocated "for making a fast start on some of the most critical problems of the impoverished region." Interest in this hitherto desolated, drought-ridden region was due to the trickle of data coming out about social unrest in a specific area in South America, second only to the entire country of Brazil itself in territorial size and population. Per capita income was $140. Wealth was concentrated in a few families, and there were news dispatches saying that this was fertile ground for the rise of another Fidel Castro. There was a paucity of penetrating political information, and the newspaper articles were sometimes oriented toward the sensational. Discovery of the Northeast by the United States was seen as a "political necessity," with a strategic role in helping in some way the continent's future course.

Just before I joined the University of Wisconsin in 1962, the university's Madison campus had received a large grant to establish the Land Tenure Center. In fact, it was because of this development that I decided to go there instead of joining the government program. Knowing my interest in South America, they asked me to draw up a proposal to study political obstacles to economic development in Northeast Brazil. My proposal, to look at "Social and Political Leadership in Northeast Brazil," was funded and I was authorized to organize a small team for initial fieldwork in summer 1963. This in turn would lead to a larger longer-term project. Dr. João Goncalves de Souza, a high official with the Organization of American States, responded to me: "Your proposal is very insightful . . . and the by-product of this research will be an action program of far-reaching dimensions."

When our team arrived in June 1963 we initially met with your rector and a number of faculty members at your University of Ceará. I should add that at this time I had not met you. (I learned only several years later that you were married to the rector's daughter.) We were based in the Institute of Anthropology at the University of Ceará and assisted by its interim director, Francisco Alencar. I was given a graduate student, Agamemnon Bezerra who spoke English and proved to be very helpful.

While our team operated in the states of Ceará and Paraiba, my most interesting research was in the small town of Pentecoste in Ceará and the surrounding rural area. We received excellent cooperation. Pentecoste was located in the heart of the horrendous drought region of the Northeast. Ten years earlier a sizable dam had been constructed by the federal anti-drought agency, DNOCS; the authorities estimated that the resulting reservoir could irrigate some 30,000 acres of valley land—yet almost nothing had been initiated to date. The water was evaporating under the hot sun.

Observers knew that there was potential for transforming the area from dire poverty to a thriving economy based on highly productive intensive truck farming, with fruit orchards and livestock, and also with hydroelectric power for small industries. When I flew across the whole Northeast region I spotted other dams and reservoirs in the same unused state. Our research question: why?

The Institute of Anthropology was interested in working with me, as was the ANCAR extension program. Our goal: to identify the obstacles preventing change and to suggest strategies needed. Seven graduate students were assigned to me as assistants to administer a questionnaire we designed together. It would be used for a random sample in the small urban sector as well as in the surrounding rural area. We prepared, as well, a leader questionnaire for open-ended separate interviews with 21 people in different positions of formal or informal influence. I soon learned that various authorities, including DNOCS, were also excited about the prospect of using the most significant untapped resource—the reservoir.

Since I sent regular diary reports on our activities to the Land Tenure Center, I was receiving enthusiastic responses on our team's efforts. While it was still early, it seemed that our Pentecoste study might really be onto something that could make a significant contribution to regional development. I returned home, shipping back 17 packages of completed questionnaires, along with documents and books, with the expectation that we'd soon return to follow up this promising beginning. Alencar was so enthusiastic that he soon flew to visit Lisa and me in Wisconsin for two days. My valuable assistant, Bezerra, arrived in Wisconsin to pursue advanced degrees. The ANCAR extension agent, Belmino, wrote me frequently that there was a unique role for Wisconsin to play and he wanted to visit our university. My last letters from Brazil to Lisa had implied that our family might soon be living in this remote area near the equator.

Lisa had been writing to me, naturally full of questions about our expected next big family move. But this conversation quickly faded away once I was back at my university. Almost immediately, our project got involved in some very unfortunate university politics. A powerful faculty member was in process of trying to take over the project. First, though, he had to get rid of the research team, and especially the person who had developed the project with the Land Tenure Center, namely me. He did this by announcing to the university authorities that while our efforts in Northeast Brazil and all the contacts we'd made had great potential, he could do a far better job of implementing the endeavor than I and our group. By marginalizing me, or even getting me out of the university altogether, this would open up his opportunity. The Land Tenure Center, however, was aware that this individual had no knowledge of Brazil and probably no ability to advance the research. It was another example of nasty university politics. The Center got cold feet, canceled the project, and withdrew the funds.

Nevertheless, the LTC was very interested in helping me to analyze and write up all the material I'd brought back. This led to the publication, *Local Political Patterns in Northeast Brazil: A Community Case Study*. The research actually produced some important findings, with large policy implications. We documented that the state deputy who represented the area in the legislature, and his brother, the vice mayor and tax collector in Pentecoste, more or less controlled local political life. Their policy was to discourage *fundamental* changes in the economic and social organization of the community and just make some small changes to combat local misery. He got public works funds to create temporary jobs, and approved minimum medical facilities. But he discouraged *real reforms* such as redistributing land, training for specialized jobs, constructing a high school, and, most significantly, preparing a leadership group with the technical skills and initiative to organize and run an irrigation system. This could transform the area, but it might also disrupt his traditional leadership.

This story could be multiplied through much of the Northeast. Why were those damned-up reservoirs of water continuing to evaporate in the hot sun, and why did American assistance often end up supporting the status quo and entrenching the power of the state deputy and his allies? It was a no-brainer as to why people in the region were anti-American!

While I continued to teach international classes, also using the new research and writing articles about Brazil and participating in conferences and seminars, I was shifting my professional interests in a major way. In the 1960s many American cities were blowing up, with inner city poverty and racial tensions threatening violence and demanding immediate attention. The University of Wisconsin, and especially UWM, which was located in Wisconsin's major urban area with explosive conditions, was being pushed "to do something." The UWM chancellor and my dean were assembling a small nucleus of faculty as a kind of think tank to begin to determine a feasible university role. In my earlier letter in this series, addressed to a dynamic inner city leader, Reuben Harpole, I detailed my involvement with him and the mounting urban issues.

A year later a fellow political scientist based in our university's Madison campus and a nationally respected scholar of problems in Latin America, heard that my promising research had been blocked. He urged me to submit a proposal to the Social Science Research Council (SSRC), a prestigious scholarly organization, to fund my return to the Northeast. Initially, my response was that I was no longer interested; my Northeast Brazil days were history. On the other hand, I felt it important to refute the negative opinions that had circulated about our team's research and me personally. Somewhat to my surprise, my new proposal to the SSRC was accepted. It built on the research begun with Pentecoste. It included bringing my family to Fortaleza for one year. Since I was now immersed in new urban initiatives, I needed a couple of years, until summer 1967, before I could free myself to return to the Northeast. While it could not have been a worse time to leave Wisconsin, I did want to make use of the grant. I also expected that the Pentecoste research would have valuable implications for the region.

On arrival at the Institute of Anthropology, I found that Professor Alencar had been replaced as director by Professor Luis Fontenelle. Little did I know then that this would soon drag me into a big-time Brazilian university political morass. I also found that my most valuable contact working in the Pentecoste area, Belmino of the extension service ANCAR, had been transferred elsewhere. Further, the mayor of Pentecoste who had promised full support had been removed. Now, in consultation with Fontenelle and you and others, we decided it would be wise to redesign the research—not eliminate Pentecoste but greatly expand our objectives.

We agreed to undertake a project that had never been attempted before: to study the leadership class of Ceará. We would focus on the six major sub-regions of the state, the so-called development poles, because studies indicated that the future economy would be built around *municipios* in these areas, along with the capital city, Fortaleza. In each place we would interview key people—important property holders, heads of companies, major political chiefs, civic leaders, leaders in the church and military.

Lisa and our two sons, Eric (eleven years old) and Steve (seven and a half), arrived in Fortaleza in September 1967. We had arranged with a Brazilian medical student, Regis Jucá, who was studying in Madison, to rent his house in Fortaleza. When we arrived we found the place in considerable disrepair and needed some time to make it livable. Several Brazilian friends urged us to find better housing, but the location was ideal. It was next door to the residence of the regional commanding general of the Brazilian army, and was patrolled around the clock by armed guards with fixed bayonets. Presumably this would enhance our safety. We were also not far from the sea; in our free time we could ride the heavy surf at fantastic beaches. Fontenelle and his wife went out of their way to help us get settled. They came around almost every day, and Elena invited us to her delicious *feijoada* dinners. A local Brazilian physician, Dr. Galba, who had studied in the United States, lived across the street and was always available for any medical question.

In contrast to some Americans stationed in Fortaleza, such as a contingent of professors and their families from the University of Arizona who were contracted to help modernize agriculture based at your university and living an almost isolated "compound" existence, we did our best to live as inconspicuously as possible. We were very aware of the visible anti-Americanism and "ugly American" sentiment prevalent in the Northeast. We opted to drive a dilapidated Brazilian jeep, not an American car.

Soon Fontenelle invited me to the Institute to meet with his staff. While during my year I had contact with everyone there, I was closest to Fontenelle, and to you and your colleague, Hélio Barros. Since your wife's father was the president of the University of Ceará, this certainly facilitated cooperation. He had a special talent for arranging international contacts and was just retiring. Fontenelle assigned you, his assistant director, to serve as my partner and closest colleague. I could not have imagined a better choice. You were a respected academic with exceptional local contacts and intimate knowledge of the Northeast.

While our year offered opportunity for a lot of innovative research, it would be hard to have envisaged the exciting time ahead of us. Since there was a dearth of political research on the Northeast, and political scientists were almost unknown, Fontenelle, you and I agreed that an appropriate starting point was to gather basic information on a number of sub-regions of this vast area. This in turn would provide the basis for analyzing the whole region and could contribute toward broad policy-making for economic and social development. Since I'd had experience working in the depressed areas of Italy and gathering data in America, which led to action to improve conditions in depressed communities, this seemed a natural lead-in for similar work in Ceará.

We would also interview a sample of Ceará's state and federal deputies, as well as leaders of agencies affecting life in the state. We felt that if we could get the people to talk and if our people were trained adequately, the research could begin to portray the state's political system. This information would be extremely useful for the many entities—local, state, national, international—which over time would contribute to real economic and social development in the region. Further, we could offer a model for others to use in dealing with much of the Northeast.

While initially I looked at this as an ambitious undertaking to be accomplished in a short time, I was excited for several reasons. It fit into the ongoing research of the Institute of Anthropology. It would be a training exercise that would likely lead to more research after I left. Above all, I had confidence in you, Paulo Elpidio, as my principal partner, along with Fontenelle. I'd offer an ongoing seminar involving faculty plus the student researchers, and we could begin to introduce political science as a field within the projected new social sciences department.

While some information was available in libraries and public agencies, most of the expected data would have to be generated through our own fieldwork. This meant leaving the Institute's offices and the university library and moving around to different parts of the state to talk to people and even face a few hardships. Fontenelle announced that the Institute was about to hire recent university graduates for this innovative research with me. After initial screening, I had lengthy interviews with a pool of people. I emphasized that this would require some tedious work and extended trips into the interior and participation in a seminar, but that it would offer a significant learning experience.

You sat in with me for most of the prospective hires. You may remember that we ended up with seven recruits from different backgrounds. Because I was learning Portuguese, and only two of them spoke fairly good English, and you were learning some English, we struggled but managed quite well. At one end of the spectrum was Wanda, a very smart, attractive and dynamic 24-year-old, about to finish her bachelor's degree in education. She taught English at the Institute in evenings and continued to help me with translating. She was by far the most radical; her student group was open to advocating violence, if required, to overthrow the "obsolescent power structure." In those days the communists in the Northeast were considered the more conservative of the political left, while the Maoists were the far left. I'm sure at the outset Wanda didn't trust me, thinking that perhaps I was an agent of the Embassy or CIA. Her friends urged her to stay clear of me, but Fontenelle vouched for me and she argued that by participating she'd be "on the inside of what really was happening."

At the other end of the spectrum we had Lino, a very bright pre-law graduate who had spent a year in Pennsylvania as an American Field Service exchange student. He spoke good English, was right wing, strongly supporting the military and traditional church. My other assistants had varied backgrounds, two of them working with the Ceará Ministry of Labor but loaned to us temporarily. They continued to be paid by the Ministry.

I agreed to pay them a modest stipend with my SSRC money, and emphasized that whatever their personal persuasions were, this project was politically neutral. As the project evolved, we all became surprisingly close, especially when local politics threatened our very existence. Each student had to choose whether to stand with me, their American scientific adviser, along with you, the administrative coordinator—or with the forces that were soon to label the project as espionage and me as an American spy. None of them left.

All the students were involved with you and me in designing the interview schedule we used and were periodically evaluating our efforts, even though none of them had much research experience.

My weekly seminar with the team was not only useful for discussing basic concepts of political science and linking intellectual discussion with organizing the research. I learned a lot about the Northeast and their own values, while they were quite enthralled with my personal background: working in postwar bombed-out Naples and meeting my future wife there in the slums, creating a refugee resettlement project in Sardinia with actor Don Murray, organizing efforts to confront poverty and racism in inner city America. They said Brazilian professors didn't get into these strange kinds of activities, and most "radicals" who favored change "just talk and argue and repeat old stereotypes but don't identify the facts or look squarely at reality for solutions." I used my halting Portuguese while the more abstract ideas received help from Fontenelle or the English–speaking students. In looking back, I'd say the most significant results were the bonding that took place that was essential for the later ordeal we all faced, and general recognition that social change would take place through creation of a new leadership class and that they had a role. I didn't know that my talks were being taped, ending up in a University of Ceará publication, *Ciência Politica e Mudança* (*Political Science and Change*).

Paulo, when you think of our year together, I'm sure you will remember the three long trips we took by bus through the state's hinterland. Since we were asking our researchers to crisscross Ceará as they collected reams of data, we ourselves had to serve as models. One trip took 10 hours each way, with a day and a half at the destination. The roads were mostly dirt and washboard. Trains were non-existent, airplanes only hit a few of the larger cities, and we saw few cars all day. The bus was the lifeline of civilization, the conveyor of people and ideas, bringing migrants from their rural mud huts to the *favelas* of Fortaleza. We crossed 3,000-foot ridges and some of the most dramatic drought areas of South America. We saw families breaking up, the youth packing their scarce possessions to leave their isolation for the big cities to seek work. We stopped in towns seldom seen by tourists. I recall one hotel that had no furniture, only four hooks on the walls for our two hammocks. Mosquitoes dive-bombed us all night.

Every *municipio* had a large television screen set up in the public square. By more or less skipping the written word in favor of the airwaves, a shift of power was taking place—from newspaper columnists to whoever controlled radio and television. We were told that even though the majority of people in the interior region were illiterate, almost everyone had a transistor radio. One radio director said he had a listening radius of 100 miles. We sometimes talked to our informants until 2:00 a.m. In one area we left two of our female researchers for two weeks to do some 62 hour-long interviews, plus descriptive community studies. Various officials wanted to loan us more workers, presumably so we could train them, but we already had our hands full.

The material we collected was absolutely fascinating. Instead of only a policy-oriented study, we had the makings of novels or movies. We met local historians who summarized the changes of the last 40 years. A local political leader told the story of a famous priest, Padre Cicero, who for 10 years ruled the area while holding the federal army at bay. He allied with a notorious bandit, pushed out elected governments that opposed him, and gained invincible power by proclaiming he was related to Jesus Christ.

On the hours riding buses, you and I learned about each other's families and your hope to study political science in Wisconsin with me. You and your wife were members of prominent families and I knew the day would come when you would replace your father-in-law as head of the university.

As part of my observation of how society worked in this part of the state, at one point I recounted to you the amazing weekend my family had experienced at a *fazenda* (aristocratic plantation) in the heart of the *sertão*:

We were invited by Glaucia, sister of the owner of our rented house, to her plantation in the interior drought area where thousands of people lived in stark poverty. Proceeding in a five-car caravan, now and then we passed a small damned-up reservoir, the water just sitting unused. We had to open and close numerous gates of grazing land, rolling up finally to a large farmhouse. We all sat on a vast veranda that wrapped around the house, and maids brought us cold drinks. We looked out onto irrigated fields and tramped around a bit of the 11,000 acres of sugar, cotton, corn, oranges, beans and pineapple. The meals were sumptuous, and most of us collapsed, satiated, in the hammocks strung up everywhere. We saw 500 head of registered cattle—majestic humped beasts—and other livestock spread around the property. Tenants with small land holdings worked halftime for the family, splitting their crop. It was only a tiny segment of the population in Northeast Brazil that controlled this plantation economy. Our leadership study would portray the region's traditional rural politics and begin to analyze what was needed as huge historic shifts were in process of taking place.

Paulo, in your lifetime I'm sure you will never forget one day in January 1968! Just as you and I and our dedicated assistants were receiving laudatory comments on our research from Professor Fontenelle and many others, we were suddenly handed a copy of *Ultima Hora*, Brazil's largest circulation daily leftist newspaper, published in Rio de Janeiro. We were jolted by the first paragraph of this front-page story attacking our project:

> The Federal University of Ceará is furnishing all the material necessary for Professor Belden Paulson of the University of Chicago and the Department of Political Science of the University of Wisconsin in order to produce an extraction of socioeconomic, political and cultural material from the state of Ceará—research whose results Brazilians will not have access to. What it is, in truth, is the renewal of the Camelot Project, destined for all of Latin America after it had been previously suspended.... It is an investigation without limits...."

The article was soon picked up by *Journal do Brasil*, one of Brazil's most important papers, and by papers elsewhere including in the Northeast. Regular news reports were also transmitted by radio and television. Rather careful groundwork had been laid among anti-American University of Ceará students, who now approached Fontenelle demanding that our project be terminated at once and that "the North American professor be asked to leave Ceará."

Several days later you and Fontenelle published in *Ultima Hora* a second article, according to the "right of reply." You denied any Camelot Project in Ceará. You wrote: "The research project on 'Political Behavior in Ceará' under our coordination is a program of investigations essentially Brazilian, executed and directed by Brazilians, and financed by Brazilians. Whoever affirms the contrary is speaking from bad faith or ignorance." While this statement was not fully accurate, it clearly indicated that your Institute of Anthropology was gearing up to defend the project and also me.

Off and on until my final departure from Ceará in August as originally planned, you and I and Fontenelle were engaged in a running battle with various forces. I can't remember if this was a new experience for you. In my case, I'd never before been attacked as an international spy, or labeled a "new James Bond." I'd never imagined that there could be such a thin line between legitimate research and espionage. And I came to appreciate even more my friendship and support from you and Fontenelle and the students.

Without too much detail, I highlight some of the events during the next months:

+ Denunciation and defense of the project on the floor of the legislature in Fortaleza.
+ Denunciation by a federal deputy from São Paulo on the floor of Congress in Brasilia, demanding a full investigation.
+ Suspension of funds by a development agency of Ceará that had committed to subsidize part of the fieldwork.

- Appointment by the rector of the University of Ceará a commission of inquiry to investigate the project, constituted of three "neutral" professors.
- Confiscation by Brazilian federal customs at the time of my departure: two boxes of my private books and some research materials, including 49 of the 210 completed interview schedules.
- Appointment by the rector of a second commission of inquiry to examine the contents of the two confiscated boxes.
- Ample coverage of the whole incident in major Brazilian newspapers, including editorials, signed columns, gossip columns, regular radio coverage in the Northeast and Europe, including Radio Moscow.

I'm sure you recall details about the Camelot Project. It had become famous in Latin America. In 1964 the Special Operations Office of the U.S. Department of the Army financed a large-scale sociopolitical study, which supposedly at the time received the single biggest grant ever awarded to a social science project—$6,000,000 for three to four years. The goal was to understand the causes of internal war in national societies and how to relieve the conditions. This was at a peak period of the Cold War when the U.S. government was very worried that what was happening in Southeast Asia might spread to Latin America. The study enlisted many respected social scientists and was to begin in Chile. Once word surfaced that funding, originally covered up, came from the military, it was generally denounced and soon canceled.

Ever since my first contact with the Northeast in 1963, I knew about the anti-American fever, that the poor Northeast was a "colony" of the richer, more developed southern Brazil. Further, since a pro-American military government took over Brazil in 1964, suspicions had crystallized about American designs. Given the tremendous needs of the region, there were numerous American initiatives, both non-profit and governmental, and while aid was encouraged, suspicions about the true objectives and funding sources were ever-present. Now this all came together in Ceará and you and I were the principal protagonists.

Over the next months there was an incredible flow of paper. You and Fontenelle spent hours preparing documents on the work of the Institute of Anthropology, the role of research toward improving conditions in the Northeast, and, given the lack of local resources, the imperative of accepting international assistance. At times the denunciations and rebuttals were so surreal that we would huddle together to observe all this and chuckle about what was becoming more like a hilarious comedy. For example, there was the day when agents visited the Institute to slice open my tennis balls and check the baskets of used toilet paper to be assured no messages were being transmitted to the State Department or CIA. However, this was also serious stuff; I noticed that Fontenelle had a pistol in his desk drawer and he made clear that under the right circumstances he'd use it.

As Institute director, Fontenelle prepared a 23-page document for the authorities detailing the research organized by you and me under auspices of the Institute, and it included details about me from my first contact with Brazil. The nine senior faculty of the Institute, including you, signed a three-page "Declaration" by the professors of the Institute describing their work, supporting your role as the administrative coordinator of this project, and confirming that this project had zero relationship to anything to do with the Camelot Project. You wrote more than one published article describing your project role and your relationship to me. You and Fontenelle also sat down with me to write a summary signed by me, entitled "Fatos Reais Relativos a Minha Presença no Ceará" (Real Facts Relative to my Presence in Ceará.) Bits and pieces of this were used at the several public hearings when I had to testify.

In this document I spelled out the essence of how we were convinced that this whole episode began with the Alencar brothers. I outlined our research in summer 1963 when we were based at the Institute of Anthropology, and how Professor Francisco Alencar, as interim director, had been very helpful. How he was so enthusiastic about the research that he visited me for two days in Wisconsin in 1965 and was already planning how we'd work together when I returned. How I was already helping the graduate student he had assigned to work with me to get a masters degree at UWM.

Everything apparently changed when Professor Fontenelle replaced Alencar as Institute director. In 1967 Fontenelle came to UWM as a visiting professor, and when he learned that I had received the SSRC grant and planned to return to the Northeast, he was enthusiastic about my basing again at the Institute of Anthropology. He also wanted to develop an official relationship between our two universities. This would involve faculty and student exchanges, and joint research beginning with me. He also insisted, and in fact was adamant, that I have no further contact with Alencar. This was not easy for me since Alencar had been so helpful in 1963 and expected to work with me again. As I looked back later, I should have figured out a way to maintain my links with Francisco socially, if not professionally. However, Fontenelle was so accommodating that I was reluctant at the time not to follow his wishes. In due course I learned the whole background story, which tied in directly with the charge that I represented the new Camelot. I was sorry that you or Fontenelle didn't fill me in with all of this sordid history. I must admit it reminded me of the unsavory politics I'd experienced at UWM after I returned from the Northeast in 1963.

Francisco Alencar's brother, José, was locally well known for attacking the university and the military government and also all American-related activities. Earlier, when the University of Ceará was discussing the need for exchanges with America, including scholarships and building up the library, José was on the front line of attack. He had held a sub-professional appointment at the university but had been removed because of his politics. It was said he was one of the most militant members of the Communist Party of Ceará. It was he who signed the original interview that led to the first *Ultima Hora* article. He also had well-placed contacts inside the University of Ceará and with the students who were using me and the research for their own purposes and as a way to attack Fontenelle.

I gradually learned that there were big stakes in play, far broader than our research project. Brazilian higher education was in the process of major reform, with various subject areas being restructured into new departments and schools. As in any university experiencing fluid change, there were power plays and plenty of jockeying. Looking to the future, one of the hottest growth areas was the social sciences, given their popularity with the students, although few courses were offered. A new faculty of social sciences would be created and a dean appointed. The current director of the Institute of Anthropology was in line for the job. However, the Alencar brothers and some others disapproved of Fontenelle and were mobilizing forces to oppose him. Since Fontenelle and his group at the Institute were in the vanguard of change, anyone opposed was potentially an Alencar ally.

My presence—one more example of "Yankee penetration"—fit perfectly into this matrix. I represented the mysterious profession of political science, which few folks knew anything about. Our formidable questionnaire to study community life and political behavior was a rarity, and although various ministries and economic development leaders and university contacts were very supportive of our research, when anyone brought up Camelot, this freshened negative memories.

Wanda had become close to me, more and more engrossed in the research and in the kind of thinking that political scientists use. She warned me that some militant student friends were "ready to act," would wait no longer to close down the research. But others (I assumed she played a lead role) were publicly asking serious questions about the insurrection:

1. What is the justification for the Commission of Inquiry? What, concretely, are its objectives? What criteria determine who is to be interviewed?
2. What specific charges are being used as a basis for the investigation?
3. What are the sources of information for denouncing this as Project Camelot?
4. Since the Institute of Anthropology defending the scientific work has publicly stated that this has nothing to do with Camelot, what evidence refutes their defense?
5. What are the central characteristics of the Camelot Project that relate to this research study?
6. What is the difference between scientific research and espionage?

Needless to say, there was no response. But you may recall, Paulo, that a tongue-in-cheek two-page paper surfaced as an indirect reflection on the investigation. A student wrote it, entitled "The Art of Espionage." Its essence:

> There's a new science of Cybernetic Information that can control the world through computers. Our first worldwide experiment begins in Ceará. Sending our material to CIA would be too obvious. We find it more devastating to send the results of our investigation to the men who gave us the information in the first place: deputies, businessmen, large property holders and government officials. There's nothing more

subversive than "hard facts." Our master is a stern taskmaster. He demands unlimited precision. He insists we go to the far corners of the state rather than sit at our desks. He requires that we constantly ask silly questions that some people, like newspaper reporters, disapprove of, like: "Are these the real facts?" or "Does this data match that from another source?" Our master is not a bureaucrat whom someone could bribe (not even by pretty girls), nor does he compliment us when we say we're 90 percent right; the missing 10 percent is cause for our ruin. Sometimes it's hard even to understand our master because he doesn't send memos in code, or even come to see us and buy us a drink. We can't even exercise our frustrations against him, our employer, because he's not flesh and blood. Our problem is that our espionage organization is a strange one: our boss lives in our minds, and he has strange aliases such as "scientific curiosity," "scientific method," and "empirical research." [This statement continued for another page discussing the facts we obtained. It ended up this way.] Good espionage, like a good general, must know the art of diversion—creating secondary explosions while we pull off the big job. Wholly by chance, we were lucky to be branded.

"Camelot Project"—a sinister operation of penetration. While people cried in the streets about Americans invading their state, we pulled off our big job. While American imperialism was being attacked from every student lair and the rector's office, we were shuffling along with our scientific investigations and then funneled the results into the broader culture.

There were a number of public hearings where many of us were called to testify. One Commission of Inquiry was established by the rector of the University of Ceará. In contrast to his predecessor, Martins Filho (your father-in-law), he was less favorable about international ties. Someone in his office was a close associate of José Alencar. He selected several distinguished academics to serve on the Commission, and I learned that José Alencar testified for seven hours. As a student, Wanda talked for two hours, the Institute's two janitors were asked about my burned toilet paper, Fontenelle spoke for three hours, and you for five hours. Finally my day arrived on May 28, 1968. You and Fontenelle urged me to give short answers. Not to say too much because they feared I might "say the wrong things." Our medical friend, Dr. Galba, accompanied me since he was well respected and spoke good English. He advised me definitely not to read my lengthy document, and to compress my testimony to half an hour. The Commission invited an official interpreter who, oddly, had studied at UWM two years earlier.

I took notes:

The Commission seemed friendly.
Member of Commission (C): What are you doing in Ceará?
BP: I'm working with the Institute of Anthropology to train students in the social sciences, and helping to develop a research project in the state.

C: Any agreement between your university and here?

BP: No formal agreement, but we've been cooperating for years.

C: How did it happen you came to Ceará?

I then began a historical account, but Dr. Galba said, "keep it short." I mentioned that 30 Brazilian professors and students were studying at one of the University of Wisconsin's campuses, indicating that there was much interest in Brazil.

BP: I directed a small research team in the Northeast in 1963. Professor Alencar visited me in Wisconsin in 1965, and Professor Fontenelle taught a seminar at UWM in 1967.

C: What is your research role now?

BP: I am technical adviser of a student research group coordinated by Paulo Elpidio de Menezes based at the Institute.

C: Anything published from your 1963 research?

BP: Yes. (I mentioned the Land Tenure Center monograph that was given to Alencar and others.)

C: Who invited you to come here now?

BP: Professor Francisco Alencar and Professor Fontenelle. The University of Wisconsin chancellor and a dean also had correspondence with the University of Ceará rector concerning my presence here.

C: Did you know about Project Camelot?

BP: Yes, I knew about what happened in Chile several years ago.

C: What were its characteristics?

BP: It was a group of persons contracted and subsidized by the U.S. Defense Department to study a plan carried out for aims of the U.S. government.

C: How does your research differ from that project?

BP: The distinctive feature of Camelot was its financing and sponsorship by the U.S. Defense Department. This research has nothing to do with the U.S. government, is financed by the SSRC and my university. I should add that all serious research, however, has certain similarities.

I made a short statement saying that although I was a busy American professor, I took a year off and my university gave permission because we are friends of Brazil and we felt the University of Ceará had potential as an important Brazilian university, and together we could carry out useful research.

I noted that when a serious scientist from the U.S. is personally attacked, this does not help our relationships. I concluded:

BP: Notwithstanding this unfortunate incident, I remain a friend of Brazil, and I ask you to include my full document in the hearing's transcript.

C: Yes, we will. Thank you for coming. We regret the stupidity of all of this, but under Brazilian law a denunciation must be investigated and cleared. (Galba and I read the transcript and signed it.)

We conversed informally for a few minutes after the hearing ended. I thanked them for their civil, responsible approach. I noted that the students working with me here compared favorably with our American graduate students. I lauded the top-quality cooperation I had from the Institute, especially my partners, Paulo Elpidio and Fontenelle. Although I noted that all of my earlier contacts had been with Francisco Alencar, who was rarely mentioned, it was his brother, José Alencar, who made the denunciation and was the source of all the trouble. Now one Commission member said he had a daughter studying in Pennsylvania. The chairman emphasized that this investigation in no way implicated me; it was simply standard procedure. They hoped it would be finished rapidly.

During this period Fontenelle was temporarily suspended as director and the Institute was closed. Luckily, I had secretly removed most of the questionnaires to my home, and you and the students came over several days a week to continue analyzing them. Signs were up around the city demanding my departure. Since the hearings were spread over several months, there was an obvious hope that the Paulson family would decide they'd had enough of the Northeast and that Fontenelle would become so sick of the turmoil that he would seek a haven for his family in Rio de Janeiro.

However, this did not happen. Fontenelle, you, and your other faculty, who had been relatively unknown, were becoming a voice to be heard in this region. For some observers you were becoming star voices of courage.

Even those professors and others who might have disagreed with your stance and tactics (which admittedly were political), agreed that the faculty must preserve its independence from the administration and from politicians. This was an important battle. It seemed that all of you were winning reluctant respect in defending a North American professor and a research effort that could bring positive and significant change to the region. I should add that at the peak of the tension Fontenelle and your group, allied with several other departments, were threatening "to call out the students into the streets."

One of my more pleasant memories is that at a critical moment when the student opposition was peaking and our research and my personal fate hung in the balance, our most radical student researcher, Wanda, stood up publicly. She risked her own neck to defend you at the Institute and me personally. Later when I left for America, she wrote in her final report:

This project was my first objective and systematic experience in the field of social science. It introduced me to a new kind of political science. It was much broader, opening up economic, sociological, and anthropological aspects of political relationships, and of the distribution and use of power in human groups. This experience showed me the possibilities of rigorous and scientific work; we could define the types of forces that determine why some people govern and others are governed, and of the possibility for individuals to become determiners of their own fate rather than have it be determined by others. It gives scientific understanding about the kind of political system that could be an instrument for effective participation in transforming society.

Paulo, you undoubtedly received the documents and final reports from the various public hearings about our research. I did see the "Official Bulletin" from the Commission of Inquiry established by the rector of the University of Ceará published in June 1968. It said that after examining all the data, there was no basis for the accusation of Project Camelot, there was no misconduct of any kind within the project or the Institute of Anthropology for studying political behavior in Ceará. And it authorized Professor Fontenelle to resume his position as Institute director.

The one unhappy result at the time of my departure was that Brazilian customs held many of the completed questionnaires and also some of my books and documents, plus the five tennis balls. The American Consulate later attempted to push the authorities to release them, but with no success. Thus while you, Paulo, arranged for the Institute to publish documents on our research, including a lengthy piece in *Revista Brasiliera De Ciência Sociais* entitled *A Classe de Liderança do Ceará* (The Leadership Class of Ceará), we lacked enough of the total data collected to do a book or the kind of comprehensive writing our work merited. I did prepare a substantial paper for the national conference of the Latin American Studies Association. Entitled "The Role of the North American Political Scientist in a Foreign Area of Social Change," I detailed the experience of our project and summarized the main findings. My last paragraph read:

> As a final word, the full research that I intended was not completed, although we produced enough good data for several publications. On the other hand, as one faculty colleague back home put it, if you had sat in your university office to diagram an imaginary project in order to understand what it's like to operate in a restless place such as Northeast Brazil, you would be hard pressed to come up with such a story as actually happened.

Lisa's best friend, Annie (Ann Louise McLaughlin), a senior editor at Harvard University Press, was telling us that we had a great book in the making in detailing the story of our adventures: my tale of "spying" and Lisa's affliction with a "voodoo" curse (soon to be described). I could also elaborate on the degree of distrust and animosity aimed at Americans compared to when I first went to postwar Europe in the early 1950s. And the need to radically reshape foreign aid to be acceptable to proud people who have not yet had "their day," yet don't want others to do things for them. And the advantage Americans have when they live somewhat comparably on the same level as their counterpart partners, not as unequal, rich "ugly Americans." Also, the extreme value of building close personal relationships with the locals so "when the shit hits the fan" there are strong allies in place. Further, the key distinctions when American researchers in anti-American environments have to explain the not-so-easy-to-analyze differences between legitimate research on sensitive topics and espionage carried out with other objectives.

When Martin Luther King was assassinated on April 4, 1968, and Bobby Kennedy on June 5, 1968, the same papers that were publishing stories on my so-called spy role now contacted me to ask my comments on these American tragedies. The prevailing Brazilian conclusion was that conspiratorial groups were in the process of wiping out our country's progressive leadership. In no way, they said, were these random incidents. I had to detail the complex civil rights struggle of many years and King's crucial role; and the admittedly unclear sequence of violent happenings befallen the Kennedy family and that family's unique place in current American history.

Paulo, throughout all the perplexing combat with the various authorities and media during these months, outside pressures pushed us—you, Fontenelle, and Hélio, alongside me—to think about and discuss the big questions that concerned us. This whole letter could easily have focused just on these issues. We were interested in the insights of social science to understand change and formulate constructive policies. All of us were interested in how political scientists study conflict between the powerful and powerless, and different possible scenarios as we looked at the future of Northeast Brazil. Given the deadlocked status quo cemented in place through centuries, what was going to happen—peaceful evolution or more revolutionary change? Keeping in mind our research project's local findings in the State of Ceará, where we identified traditional leaders and reformers and also potential revolutionaries, what conclusions could we draw for this one state, not to mention for the political system of the whole region?

I was delighted when our discussion stimulated you and Hélio to consider joining Bezerra in Wisconsin to continue this discussion, as well as being able to pursue advanced work in political science. Once I returned home I arranged for both of you to be admitted into the graduate program of my department at UWM and to receive an assistantship, which would entail some financial assistance. I was happy that Hélio joined our program in 1969 for two years and received a master's degree. He assisted me with some classes. Unfortunately, even though all local arrangements for you had been finalized, you were not able to make it. In any event, you came to Wisconsin later on behalf of your university. I should add that Wanda also discussed her eagerness to come to study in Wisconsin, but this never materialized.

While many years have passed—half a century—you may remember that along with the Camelot Project events, my family (especially Lisa) encountered on a very personal level the mysteries of the local *macumba* (the voodoo of the Northeast). This had nothing directly to do with our research, but the experience was invaluable in helping me to understand the functioning of the different population strata in this part of the country. You and Fontenelle were very helpful in explaining the social complexities, some of which fall completely outside the mainstream culture. Looking back now, I'd like to summarize Lisa's unique experience, which was to have considerable influence on our lives.

After we'd been settled in Fortaleza for a number of months, Lisa came down with a crippling headache, paralysis of her extremities, and the sense that she was "going crazy." This was terrifying. It got so bad that I seriously considered sending her and our two boys back to America. I asked the advice of our Brazilian friend, Dr. Galba, whether she could be suffering from a heart attack or stroke. Or maybe she'd gotten too much sun. Or, when recently she'd been pressed to perform with her cello in a public concert, maybe the pressure was too much. Galba examined her thoroughly and said there was nothing *physically* wrong. He told us, however, that after studying in the U.S., and then practicing for a long time in the Northeast, he knew that many people had maladies that could not be explained by modern medicine. Besides being in pain and partially paralyzed, Lisa couldn't tolerate anyone coming near her.

One Sunday evening a local "spiritist" practitioner showed up in our garden. (Spiritism, as you no doubt know, is a distinct religious sect imported from France, specifically focused around inviting the spirits of the dead to help with problems of their congregations.) José was visiting our household helper, Maria. I should say a word about Maria. When we first arrived, Fontenelle had urged us to hire a helper to assist in dealing with all the intricacies of indigenous customs and culture, running a house and fixing utilities that constantly failed. We'd had similar useful help in other overseas locations where we'd worked. Maria grew up in the *sertão* (drought region) with 15 brothers and sisters. Her mother died when she was nine and she was forced to work in the blistering fields picking rice, beans and cotton, giving her almost nonexistent wage to her father. Her mother had been a dressmaker and Maria's burning ambition was someday to own a sewing machine and to take up this work. She was 15 when she took the risk of traveling alone to Fortaleza to hire out as a maid.

When Maria first came to us she kept mostly to herself, but gradually she opened up to Lisa, spilling all the traumatic details of her life. Lisa became her surrogate mother, and Maria confided how she had actual frequent (very frightening) night visitations from a dead sister. Through a girlfriend, she had gotten to know José, the spiritist, who it turned out was a gifted medium able to access "the other side." He was part of a local spiritist group in an outlying *favela* and had helped to explain her apparitions.

I understood that most big cities in Brazil had their *favelas*, or slum areas. Fortaleza's were in a vast no man's land where authority rarely penetrated. There were minimal public utilities, such as a functioning waste system; rivers of sewerage flowed through rutted paths in the sand dunes. In many parts there were no lights, no electricity. Hundreds of little huts spreading across the dunes along the sea formed shantytowns where stark poverty reigned.

José's spiritist group met in a primitive shack in one *favela*, and in another the devotees of the local *macumba* worshipped and practiced.

We learned that *macumba* was a religion mixing the worship of African deities (brought over with the slave trade) with that of the Portuguese Catholic saints. We got to know the high priestess of the *macumba*. By day Raimunda worked as a maid for the local Peace Corps director, but in the other part of her life she was the powerful matriarch of her *favela*. She found jobs for people, and commanded total allegiance. Lisa and I were curious about the exotic *macumba* rituals and Raimunda invited us to come watch. Lisa's descriptive few words give the flavor.

We arrived at the *macumba* hut in the sand dunes in almost complete darkness. Shadowy figures in long white dresses or shirts were darting around and filing into the little building adorned with pictures of St. George slaying the dragon. The ceremony began and people (women on one side, men on the other—no children allowed) were kneeling, crossing themselves, clapping. Raimunda, presiding at the alter, led the chanting and singing, which began with the boys on the bongo drums, shakers and triangles stationed at the front. The voices sometimes pulsated with responsive Hail Marys, sometimes burst into wild hymns, and at times resembled the primitive African chants with which *macumba* is linked. . . . An assistant priestess produced a pot of burning incense, and went around swinging it in everyone's face. Each participant rushed to inhale the smoke and get even dizzier. Raimunda, fortified with a bottle of *cachaça* (Brazilian rum), shouted her rituals at the alter, and then invited the congregation, one by one, to come up to be blessed and then they were whirled off to dance in a frenzied trance until they dropped unconscious on the dirt floor. . . .

Returning our discussion to that Sunday evening when José met Maria in our garden, he suddenly said to her: "There's someone sick here, with a very bad headache?" Yes. "It's especially bad around the eyes?" Yes. He concentrated for a while. "Is it the signora?" Yes. "Has she ever visited a *macumba*?" Yes, occasionally. "And was there some dispute with the high priestess?" Later, Lisa expanded on José's correct insights. She had borrowed Raimunda's sewing machine, then, as a thanks, put money into the collection plate the next night we visited her ceremony. Raimunda apparently thought Lisa's money was a routine offering for the *macumba* and that she—supposedly a rich American—should have given more for use of the machine. Lisa remembered a sudden flash of anger. José guessed that in that moment of anger Raimunda had put the "evil eye" on Lisa. She had called down a departed soul that had died from a terrible pain in his head, and that entity was now attached to Lisa. It was a punishment, not necessarily meant to do her in but to cause suffering.

José explained that the best way "to exorcise the spirit" was to go to the next *macumba* session, greet Raimunda in a friendly way, drop a modest contribution in the plate, and then make an excuse to leave after just ten minutes. Since Lisa was not eager to return to the *macumba*, an alternative was for her to attend José's next spiritist meeting where he officiated.

I must admit that I had serious questions about all this chatter about the *macumba* and intervention from dead spirits. At the same time, since Lisa was in desperate straits, we agreed: "Let's give José's spiritist talents a try," I said. Our whole family and Maria piled into our old jeep and headed to his shanty in the sand dunes.

Lisa described what happened:

> The hut was jammed with sweating, tattered humanity on the benches in the rear part. A bar up front separated the mass of people from a large round table covered with a white embroidered cloth. A dozen or so mediums sat around the table, hands covering their eyes. José spotted us and came back immediately to get my exact name. Then he beckoned me to come down and sit next to the table, inside the bar. First there were three short sermons by the pastor. Then the real business of the evening began. José, as chief medium, moved around the table, touching each of the mediums lightly on the head. This immediately caused them to tremble violently, and often they shrieked and wept like babies. What apparently was happening was that spirits were being summoned to "come down" and enter one of the mediums. José, on catching messages, would call out to the congregation, "Who is there here called Marina? There is a spirit who wants to talk with Marina." This went on for quite a while, and then the final bell sounded, the kerosene lanterns were turned up, and the entire assemblage broke out in a long earnest hymn. The mediums were instructed to lay their hands down on the table, and they were brought up to full consciousness. I had no idea as to whether my "case" had been pleaded.

By now our boys and I had had enough of the strange doings taking place in José's fragrant enclave and went out to wait in the jeep. When Lisa finally emerged from the hut, she asked Maria what had happened. Maria asked whether she had noticed a curtained door off to the side of the room. Lisa recalled seeing a steady stream of congregants filing into that hidden space and deep groans and sharp wailing noises issuing. It was there, Maria said, that the really serious patients were being treated by the spiritist doctor, and that my bad spirit had been dealt with there. It had been persuaded to depart. As we drove, Lisa noticed, to her amazement, that her headache was gradually lifting, and by the time we arrived home she could move her hands and feet freely for the first time in weeks. She actually felt normal again.

I called Dr. Galba to summarize what had happened. He said there was no medical explanation. One doesn't know what really occurs in these circumstances. The bottom line was that Lisa felt more or less cured. The puzzling question: was this whole episode a coincidence, or power of suggestion, or was it truly an exorcism? The reason didn't really matter; enough that a healing did occur.

Paulo Elpidio, when I write this story after 50 years, I wonder if it sounds as incredible to you as it did to me in 1968 when we were riding through the sand dunes in the jeep and Lisa told us she was miraculously healed. This is not the usual social science we're used to, but obviously something to be reckoned with. When Lisa describes this experience to people back home, she emphasizes that when so many people—from all classes—believe naturally in the closeness and communication with "that other world," as they do in Brazil, the veil is definitely thinner. When she returned home to the more materialistic, less credulous United States, the atmosphere felt entirely different.

Before I sign off, I must share something with you I'd not thought much about until I wrote this letter. As noted earlier, my time in Brazil only encompassed one summer (1963) and then later, one full year (1967-68). You could rightly say that these were small specks in my long life. Nevertheless, these experiences had major unexpected impacts. They were unforgettable turning points in the lives of my entire family.

After my team's successful study in the Northeast in 1963, I was preparing to return soon to undertake a research and development project that might take several years. The Land Tenure Center had already committed financing. My international work in the university would continue. And my family assumed we were about to move south. However, all of this changed almost overnight.

As I reported early in this letter, I learned on returning to the university that a powerful person was in process of taking control of the money and the project, and for this to happen he tried to wield his power to get me out. While this did lead to cancellation of the project, it also had a significant impact on me personally. For a period of time I had to shift my energies away from further international research in Brazil. While I did return there in 1967-68, I had already been pushed by my university to create a major response to the looming national and local urban crisis. With other associates, I established its first department dealing with central city poverty and racism.

During our year in the Northeast in 1967-68, Lisa's traumatic contact with *macumba* and the high priestess Raimunda, her close affinity to the traumas of our helper Maria, and "cure" through José's spiritism, opened up a whole new world of interest for her. Not long after returning to Milwaukee, the unique experiences in Fortaleza influenced her to join forces with a group forming a new entity, Psy-Bionics. This involved teaching and writing about altered states of consciousness and exploring the parameters of parapsychology. It led to contacts with many nationally known figures in this field, which, in turn, brought her to an intimate experience at Findhorn, the famous spiritual community in Scotland. The Findhorn immersion led her to take a lead role in creating a similar "intentional" community in Wisconsin—High Wind. Through High Wind we, with many others, helped to open up alternative scenarios and demonstrations in our region that pointed to possible future directions and imperatives for our culture.

While my urban work and Lisa's efforts dealt with different subject matter, they were interrelated in various ways. Without the Brazil events of 1963 and 1967-68, there would have been no new university urban department and no High Wind. Paulo, it's my guess that until reading this letter, you had no idea of the deep ramifications of our time in Brazil with you.

What an amazing moment it would be if we were to meet again in our now advanced years, to remember our unforgettable adventures together. We could see in retrospect how one unexpected event led to the next, with huge impacts on both our lives!

Mystic David Spangler connects
future vision with mainstream university

Dear David,

After Lisa's three weeks at Findhorn in fall of 1976, more and more often I began hearing the name "David Spangler." She noted that at the major conference there your talks about the "New Age" and "World Crisis and the Wholeness of Life" were some of the most compelling. Several months later when I met Findhorn cofounder, Peter Caddy, who was lecturing in Chicago, he emphasized that during your three years in the community you exponentially enriched its spiritual depth and educational role, as well as contributing to its broad planetary focus. Now and then we were even beginning to hear comments in passing (obviously not too seriously) to the effect that you might have something to do with the "Second Coming."

Needless to say, when I first met you in October 1977 at your weekend workshop at Lake Geneva, Wisconsin, my usual skepticism reared its conspicuous head. However, when we played some Ping Pong to break the ice, I must admit that by the end of the three days I was very open to seeing more of you. At that point I barely knew what questions to ask, and since there were some 30 people attending the workshop, we had only limited contact. You were in your early thirties, clearly with no "big head" or arrogance, and we sensed that in your low-key way you were skilled in conveying thoughtful comments that seemed to emerge from some inner reservoir of mysterious power— but always with a light touch and abundant, self-deprecating humor. You never spoke with notes.

That fall when we organized a pretty far-out university course, "Planetary Survival and the Role of Alternative Communities," we invited you to lead one class during the 15 weeks, and also to present a lecture on campus. Little did I, or presumably you, have any idea of the flurry of events that were to follow. Now, after all these years, I use this letter to you to recount briefly the essence of what happened, much of which was outlined in my published memoir of a decade ago.

The story obviously begins with Lisa's short but intense personal immersion at Findhorn, the renowned intentional community in northern Scotland. The 1970s may have been the legendary community's spiritual heyday when you were there. Some 250 residents from around the globe were not only designing a model of "the good life" but were trying to live it every day.

As a mystic and teacher you were articulating Findhorn as a seed point for a coming new era. There would be a "fundamental change of consciousness from one of isolation and separation to one of communion and wholeness, to build a future different from what we already know or expect." In the introduction to your book, *Revelation: The Birth of a New Age*, you wrote that the New Age is "an expression of a highly flexible and creative consciousness, freed from time and space, and living in the moment attuned to the Divine Will. This may be a definition, but we have no definitive blueprint for how to make the New Age a reality, at least not yet."

I should add that, years later, around 1990, you told us that your work had "refocused itself from the idea of collective emergence embodied in the best of the New Age movement to exploring the emergence of the sacred individual." This, in turn, you continued, "led to the development of 'Incarnational Spirituality,' which has been my focus since 2001." Then by 2016 you said you had further shifted from "researching the incarnational process of the individual to exploring the relationship of an individual to the planetary soul or 'Gaia'—Gaian consciousness." You said that this "deepens the work of Incarnational Spirituality and illumines how we as individuals are co-creative participants in the incarnation of the world."

I wrote you that, "in my own mind I felt that in the relationship of the two of us we always merged all three emphases as one integral approach in defining how we see the world and interpreting our own work. I never gave up on the pioneering thinking you brought in defining the New Age as the emergence and evolution of a collective consciousness, while also interrelating this to the role of the sacred individual, as well as to our societal push toward a planetary consciousness." You quickly responded: "Yes, I agree; although I separate out the periods of my life according to where the major emphasis was; all three elements have always been present and part of who I am and what I have to offer. We did indeed blend them nicely in the work we did together in Milwaukee, a time I continue to treasure."

Returning to Lisa. Once back home in Wisconsin after Scotland, she was a different person than the Lisa I'd known during our previous 23 years together. I'd never seen her so fired up. Clearly, she didn't want to be dragged back from the heights of New Age euphoria into Wisconsin's mainstream culture.

We arranged for her to report on Findhorn at a major upcoming conference in Chicago that featured E. F. Schumacher, author of the recent best seller, *Small Is Beautiful*. We signed up a room for 15 people, but then found 400 attendees lined up expectantly in the hall for her presentation, the second largest audience of the 2,300 attendees after Schumacher's. I invited my dean, who was fascinated to see this astonishing public interest. Since this was a time of declining university enrollments, he urged me to organize similar events at our University of Wisconsin campus.

Although this is distant history, it's my guess, David, that you remember our inviting Peter and Eileen Caddy to speak about Findhorn in Milwaukee in June 1977. We had no idea what would happen, but just in case, I secured the largest university space available. Some 1,200 people showed up from all walks of life. Besides the expected "seekers" and counter-cultural types, we saw folks from business, government, and community groups, as well as students and faculty. While the Caddys discussed the future of our culture and current crises we faced (such as the world blowing itself up as the culmination of the Cold War), they mainly focused on Findhorn as a visionary model for the future, with broad planetary applications. Since it was obvious they were generating a wild outpouring of enthusiasm, Lisa and her associates garnered the names and addresses of all the attendees, a terrific list for subsequent communications. The Caddys stayed with us for a week and we mapped out possible lines of prospective collaboration between Findhorn and our group in Wisconsin. While here, we drove them out to our 46-acre farm 50 miles north of Milwaukee. Standing near the big barn, Eileen recounted a vision of "tent stakes being driven slowly into the ground, with a group coming together in a steady work rhythm, people close to nature, spreading and living a new consciousness."

You know the next chapters. I received university approvals to line up a series of seminars that drew not only academics, but people from around Wisconsin and the region and country. Our first essential action was to enlist you and your Findhorn colleague, Milenko Matanovic, to teach credit and non-credit courses with me. You and Milenko moved to Milwaukee in summer 1978 with your families and other colleagues (now calling yourselves "Lorian"). After two intense years you shifted to Madison where you remained for four more years before returning to the West, this time the Seattle area. Our work together, however, with teaching and other collaborations, continued well into the 1990's, and we've remained in contact.

By spring 1978 I figured it was time for me to visit Scotland with Lisa. She returned to Findhorn as a working guest in the community and participated in a workshop, "Creating a Centre of Light" with Peter Caddy. This soon proved invaluable for us in Wisconsin. I enrolled in "Experience Week," an in-depth look at Findhorn's philosophy and its practical functioning. I spent time with the community's key "focalisers" (described as those who coalesce the energies and ideas rather than issuing orders). I came to feel what it was like to live at Findhorn, participating and sharing on many levels. There were "attunements" before each activity, silent meditations in the sanctuary, exercises to build group cohesion, and for half of every day we threw our energy into community work projects such as food growing and meal preparation. All of this tied into the wholeness of the community vision and understanding the mission of global outreach.

The two focalisers of my group of 15 embodied a lot of love and knew exactly how to introduce us to some very new ideas and ways of being. I sought out individual community members for discussions on the unorthodox governance methods Findhorn created, and the underlying meaning of the work and its interrelationship with nature and "nature beings." I was especially interested in the life of this community and its larger planetary connection. I spent time with a participant in my group who was a top administrator of a hospital in New York. We agreed that if he tried to introduce the Findhorn model in his workplace, he'd probably last about a week. I concurred that as a professor in my university's institutional setting, I'd likely face similar consequences.

Going back to the sequence of events in Wisconsin, let's quickly trace the early steps on which you and I built our subsequent collaboration. Rue Hass, a recent Findhorn resident (and Lisa's confidante there) and a teacher by profession, came to see us in Wisconsin in January 1977. We arranged for her to speak to a university class of faculty and students about the concept of intentional community. In February Dorothy Maclean, a Canadian and spiritual icon and cofounder of Findhorn along with the two Caddys, hosted a weekend workshop in Milwaukee with her young assistant, Freya Conger, part of your education group from Findhorn. Milenko Matanovic and his vivacious wife Kathi, gave a concert in Milwaukee bringing songs they and you had composed at Findhorn. (You had called yourselves "The New Troubadours," with popular recordings produced in the community.) These events created strong interest and curiosity about Findhorn, and many folks wanted to learn more. As mentioned above, the conference in Chicago that gave Lisa opportunity to describe Findhorn to an overflow audience took place in spring 1977. All this activity led to the Caddys' talk at the university in June.

Immediately after Peter and Eileen left, I sat down with two open-minded university colleagues in charge of off-campus education. I suggested that the time was ripe to offer a series of fully-developed courses for undergraduate and graduate credit (or for non-credit), but which would not easily fit into any academic department or discipline. The purpose: "To become more aware of the interconnectedness of everything on our planet, and what we must challenge about our cultural and technocratic conditioning. We'd discuss the ecological and spiritual crises we face, and what in our current society might not be viable. We'd test our courage to let go of entrenched paradigms, belief systems, lifestyles. We'd look at examples of creating communities that embrace new thinking, and demonstrations of technologies more appropriate to a world of diminishing natural resources." I'd take responsibility for the academic quality. My colleagues agreed that if this "trial balloon" worked it could pave the way for more such innovative offerings.

The first seminar, "Planetary Survival," didn't meet on campus but in the storefront Village Church downtown, whose "with-it" minister also enrolled. Beginning in September 1977 and extending for 14 weeks, we met from 6:30 to 9 P.M. one night a week, often extending for another hour. As a result of Lisa's list from the Caddy talk, as well as from the university catalog, the first night we found people forming a long line around the block to register. We ended up with 125 "students," some for credit, some non-credit. They were of all ages, from 17 to 70. Some drove up from Chicago and they came from all around Wisconsin. The first half of each session provided a philosophical framework, while the second half showcased examples of practical applications. As mentioned earlier, the invited speakers included you and Milenko, along with a cross-section of new thinkers drawn nationally.

In the summer before the class began, Lisa and I and two alternative builder friends very interested in ecology visited the projects of the New Alchemy Institute. This was an international non-profit organization with demonstrations of very innovative technologies. At the Schumacher conference, its cofounder, biologist John Todd, told us about their exciting experimental work with renewable energy. The "bioshelter," aka the Ark, was a structure designed to provide its own energy and climate, purify its own wastes biologically, and grow food for its residents. They had found funds to build two Arks: a smaller one at their home base on Cape Cod in Massachusetts, and a larger one on Prince Edward Island in Canada—the latter supported by the Canadian Government and inaugurated by the prime minister.

We read the sophisticated literature about these projects and decided it was imperative to go see them and learn more. The four of us set out for points East, visiting both Arks and absorbing details about their construction and operation. Soon afterwards we invited their architect, David Bergmark, and the New Alchemy agronomist, Linda Gilkeson, to Wisconsin to assist us in designing and finding money for a similar project in the Midwest. Both had given talks about renewable energy and the concept of bioshelters at the Planetary Survival seminar.

The energy generated by all these activities was unbelievable. People poured out of the woodwork to volunteer—for whatever. They wanted to be involved in what they saw as presaging a new culture. The healthy attendance and positive feedback from the class, not to mention the sizable income generated, were pleasing to the university. Your presence as a lecturer, and the workshop at Lake Geneva, as well as your informal meetings at our house where you were staying, inspired people to learn more. You were spreading the idea that a special consciousness was emerging in the Midwest that might be more pure and grounded than on either coast. We heard people saying that you were "years ahead of your time," and the comment, "If you're sufficiently evolved or at a certain point in awareness, you're ready for David—otherwise, forget it!" Of course, a few people shook their heads and told us you were "out to lunch," that you were so removed from familiar mainstream thinking that they wanted nothing to do with you.

In preparation for you and Milenko and your families arriving in summer 1978, we began discussing the first university course we'd teach together in the fall. Given the huge attendance at the Caddy talk and also the Planetary Survival class, I expected to find strong university support, as with the two university colleagues I mentioned above. At this time the institution was definitely into the numbers game, to assure needed income. For years I'd been teaching seminars in the political science department, and in one sequence had offered an innovative series that focused on inner city leadership. Since this mostly minority population had felt completely disempowered and even disenfranchised, my aim was to enhance their understanding of how the political system was supposed to function and how they could broaden their own political participation. These classes had generated strong attendance and received enthusiastic university support.

Now we were embracing a new theme: to see how far we could go in redefining politics. Our approach was significantly different from conventional political science. While you and Milenko and I designed the course, we enlisted an array of smart thinkers, including a number who were active in the political system, such as elected officials disillusioned with the politics they knew. (This was 40 years ago; many of today's elected politicians are even more disillusioned.)

I discussed this new course with the political science department, but eventually decided to work with one of the university's more creative departments, Cultural Foundations of Education, located in the UWM School of Education. Its chair, Richard Cummings, was an old friend with international experience somewhat similar to mine, and sensitive to new trends sweeping the world. His department was to host and provide credit for many of my subsequent offerings.

Before he could sign off on this seminar, it had to clear the university vice chancellor's office. This additional filter was the only time this ever happened in my 35 years of University of Wisconsin teaching.

We named our course "New Dimensions in Governance: Images of Holistic Community." In looking back, this seminar was probably the most influential class I offered at this point in my life. It laid the groundwork for founding our intentional community, High Wind. It linked in with the New World Alliance, a significant endeavor coalescing nationally with a new vision of politics. It planted seeds for an initiative that a decade later led to a national consultation to create a holistic think tank, held at the United Nations Plaza in New York. This also provided a push to begin preparing the intellectual and value framework for subsequent teaching on the subject of building a sustainable world.

The class met two nights a week for 15 weeks, beginning in September and ending in mid-December. Once again we met off-campus, at Village Church in downtown Milwaukee. Attendance was a cross-section of the local community and the region. People registered for graduate or under-graduate credit or non-credit. Despite frequent bad weather, attendance was almost perfect. Years later, people still referred to this class.

The curriculum, stating our purpose, was based on the opening paragraph of the publicity brochure:

> To explore social and political concepts related to the idea of people becoming more sensitive to resource scarcities and preservation of the earth, more aware of the

possibilities for new forms of human interaction and connectedness—on the premise that changed individual priorities can lead to changed ways of ordering society.

We introduced your concept of "holocracy" that you'd been discussing with us. I was trying to fit your ideas into more accepted political science terminology. Your starting point was that a "new consciousness was emerging in the world and that the power in each one of us could transform the world and bring into being a New Age." Your own values were intrinsic to this non-physical dimension of life—of spirit. You used the term "Limitless Love and Truth." I needed to make sure that this "spiritual" dimension remained intact yet outside of our publicized vocabulary. Our public university required strict observance of separation of Church and State.

We agreed that among the basic ideas of the modern western tradition is individual self-sufficiency. This is fulfilled through a societal process fueled by conflict between individuals and groups pursuing their own selfish interests. A general balance of power is essential to provide some equilibrium among diverse groups so that no one individual or group or interest completely dominates. In conventional political science, politics, in essence, is the struggle for power in allocating scarce resources. Now, looking at the ecological and spiritual crises we were facing, a very different approach was called for.

Your idea of holocracy went back to the ancient and medieval periods with the concept of the "universal community." That vision of governance was based on "wholeness," where nothing was ultimately separate. Instead of the contemporary western Newtonian image of the political and social universe made up of interacting but individual "atoms," the individual parts created a wholeness that was more than the sum of the parts. This actually built on contemporary research in quantum physics, ecology, holistic health, and many other new fields actually linked to those ancient ideas, where everything is interrelated and the parts and the whole benefit mutually from each other. Holocracy here meant rule by and in the interest of the whole, which begins on the level of consciousness but then translates into forms of varying complexity on the levels of the individual, the local community, the nation and planet. Holistic governance sees everything as interrelated and interdependent; nothing is ultimately separate or isolated from anything else.

You and Milenko and I soon found we had a tiger by the tail. Our course objective was to translate this model of holistic thinking to the practical level of everyday living in today's politically off-kilter value system. We spent hours thinking through the questions that quickly surfaced in our smart class. For example, in the actual exercise of power and authority, what guarantee is there that decision-makers will function holistically instead of continuing to merely serve selfish interests? What would have to happen for a political system to become more sensitive to holistic governance, transcending the prevailing narrow self-serving partisanship? Is it even possible to produce enlightened governance that feeds the needs and interests of the *whole* community? Our critics argued that this is the dream world of naïve idealists. "Wholeness" merely ends up in some new form of control where those exercising power imply they are serving the whole while in fact they are autocrats. Typically, this situation descends

---

into some form of totalitarianism, as we've seen throughout history and which was exemplified in the 20th century.

Since this integral relationship between consciousness and holistic decision-making is the essential factor in creating holocracy, are there strategies to be designed that will elevate the level of consciousness? This would have to apply in at least some minimal way to the population generally, and most specifically to those of us who may be selected to govern. We agreed that this would be the central challenge to explore in our seminar.

Before going further as we prepared for this course on a new politics, I'd like to share with you a background personal note. This is because it may not be only "by chance" that we came to work together. In your early days in Wisconsin, we spent a lot of time together. I was trying to understand where you were coming from and I'm sure you were attempting to figure me out. We were a couple of fairly strange characters! Your public image was of one who dwelled in the world of spirit, of transpersonal realities, of a new kind of awareness. Presumably my public persona was someone who operated "on the ground" as a practical problem-solver in the material world, dealing with tangible projects, systems and institutions. In our time together, a complementary relationship evolved where we were learning to comprehend each other's starting points.

Your image of New Age made sense to me: where it was understood that greed and selfishness and lust for power had gotten in the way of creating a society that was fair and caring of everyone, of all life. This could extend to envisioning a new kind of politics. That consciousness could begin to move toward your limitless love, a term you liked but which political scientists would never use. In the real world this could translate to moving from narrow isolation—every man for himself—to a concern for the larger common good. In other words, this implied *Community*. My past work with dire poverty and abandoned refugees in Europe, and then later in America's inner cities, was always to find strategies to build community. This required redefining policies that benefited only the few to decision-makers caring for the many. It required people working together, and refocusing "interest" from the narrow to the broad—ultimately to the entire community—be it a small group or a town or nation or even the world.

When I was growing up, I didn't have much allegiance to formal religion. But my mother, who was wise and understood me well, and also was very spiritual, found that I more or less understood when she discussed "Spirit." She spoke of how an awakened "consciousness" was a path to Spirit and to love—the opposite of selfishness and interest only in oneself. It also meant that while the material world where we lived was very "small," the world of Spirit was very large. It was also full of mystery. In the realm of Spirit everything was possible because there were no boundaries. I sensed there were "miracles" happening all the time. They might not be miracles we learned about in the Bible but they were things that simply happened because our very limited understanding that had been nurtured in the material world could not grasp the mysterious basis of this other kind of reality, the world of Spirit. I had found in my work life that sometimes I'd face problems that looked absolutely impossible. Of course I was depending on the usual economic and political and other linear methodologies that people use to solve problems. Yet sometimes the impossible became possible. Apparent "miracles" did happen. Since there was no rational explanation, I concluded that when "mysterious forces" came into play, for lack of other explanation, strings were being pulled in the world of Spirit.

In my teaching and often in my work dealing with practical problem solving, we've often used the term "transformation" when we're dealing with fundamental change. We emphasize the term "fundamental" since most change is not *fundamental*. My understanding of transformation refers to conversion from one basic state to another—which is something altogether different from a small, surface-level shift. Sometimes we can comprehend significant change by using scientific methods developed empirically that have coalesced into proven "laws." For example, in the physical world we know about fundamental change such as when a caterpillar changes into a butterfly, or a tadpole becomes a frog. However, in the human world fundamental change is harder to understand because we are also dealing with values. This ties into "paradigm shifts," using Thomas Kuhn's concept (defined in his book *The Structure of Scientific Revolutions*) where we change our basic way of perceiving, thinking and doing that is associated with a particular vision of reality. In the huge body of research on this subject, a mind-bending source I've used is a pair of seminal articles on "The Coming Transformation" in the *Futurist* magazine in 1977. This was published just when we were doing our class and I had much contact with the author, futurist and Stanford professor, Willis Harman. His research and analysis concluded that modern industrial societies in today's historical period are in the throes of fundamental change, which may not be too different from past great shifts, such as the movement from hunters and gatherers to agriculture, and then to the industrial age and the information age, and perhaps in the near future to the age of artificial intelligence and robots.

As we explored the meaning of your term, "New Age," I sensed that "Transformation" had a very similar connotation. Both involved a fundamental change of values that would in turn lead to a reordering of our social culture. Presumably this includes a new kind of politics as well, where a change of consciousness produces more holistic human attitudes and interactions. YOUR starting point is personal consciousness, which in turn leads to a reordering of societal relationships, while MY starting point is societal relationships that will require a change of consciousness. It would seem that working toward societal Transformation and a New Age are very similar; the end point of both is cultural change brought about through change of consciousness. Many of our efforts together, such as the New Dimensions seminar, were small-scale experimental efforts to think through and participate in this kind of historic change that we are all part of today, and working with our respective terminologies.

Returning to our seminar, as a starter we asked the class to see itself as a "mini-community" where all of its actions are carried out for the benefit of the whole class. Intellectually, in various talks and discussions, we examined wholeness from multiple perspectives, using ideas and models drawn from selected literature and practical examples. We organized the class with its 80 participants so that everyone would have ample time to participate in small interest groups. These were: Envisioning the Organization of a Residential Community (specifically through the vehicle of creating a bioshelter); The Arts (mounting a theatrical production); Holistic Health (conceiving an innovative clinic involving integrative medicine); Planning a New Age Business (such as a vegetarian restaurant serving foods grown naturally and locally); Designing Educational Curricula (learning for the New Age); Communication (a program for the university's radio station, which offered us an opening); and A New Politics Initiative (several class participants already held fairly high-level political positions). There were three goals for each group: participants would be aware of their process of working together within a holistic framework; they would design a specific project as a springboard for cooperative relationships that could be tested in the real world; and as a final product, each group would put together a paper or some creative project that exemplified its interpretation of holocracy.

While the seven interest groups came up with interesting projects, it was the environmental group that came up with perhaps the most significant outcome. It concentrated on creating a community on the land, and building an environmentally energy-efficient and revolutionary bioshelter using the model of the New Alchemy Institute. It was these ideas that later were largely implemented in the founding of the High Wind community.

Our seminar premise was not only to meet as a class with its flow of information and co-created ideas. We wanted everyone to have an experience of practical holism in action. We felt that the most relevant examples we knew about were the "alternative communities," also known as "intentional communities," scattered around the United States and the world. We used the term "alternative" in the sense that these communities challenged mainstream values in fundamental ways. They were thoroughly examined in the book, *Builders of the Dawn* by Corinne McLaughlin and Gordon Davidson. These veterans of community living, who met with us several times, had lived at Findhorn, had founded the Sirius intentional community in Massachusetts, and in writing their book had visited over a hundred such communities.

They noted that although these communities were widely diverse, they shared certain characteristics: planetary awareness of the oneness and interdependence of all life; commitment to psychological/spiritual growth and taking this out to serve society; dedication to healing the earth and living in harmony with nature; reducing consumption and employing renewable energy; commitment to non-violence; and racial and gender equality. While they might or might not have an explicit "spiritual" focus, the commitment of the communities studied was to a conscious emphasis on holistic, benign thinking and practice.

Since you and Milenko had detailed personal knowledge of Findhorn after living and leading there, and Lisa and I also had some Findhorn experience, we regularly made reference to this world-famous example. One of our outside speakers was Jim Maynard, an attorney living at Findhorn at the time. He articulated in detail how holistic governance worked with Findhorn's 200-odd residents. Later in the class we set aside two weeks for each participant to go visit an alternative community; we recommended 10 across the country for possible study.

As an immediate follow-up after the class, we scheduled a special opportunity for up to 30 participants to spend four to eight weeks at Findhorn in spring 1979. They'd be able to test all the ideas we had explored. The amazingly positive feedback from this trip resulted in the formation of an enthusiastic group that said they were ready for "next steps," whatever form these might take.

Prior to the Findhorn trip, we offered two non-credit classes to further deepen the understanding of transformation. Your class, David, "Esoterics: The Relationship Between Spiritual Forces and Creative Living," explored the nature of the esoteric tradition; the creative hierarchies (such as spiritual beings; the psychology of magic; the laws of manifestation; the role of meditation and prayer; and the development of a group mind). Milenko's class, "Performing the Future— Transformation and the Arts," showed how the arts can bring out the highest potential for oneself and the community by blending service, creative communication, and celebratory ritual.

All of these endeavors were surprisingly popular. A group of more than 50 folks bonded and registered for everything we offered. After a while we began to hear this refrain: "We love every course but we're getting 'seminared out.' We need to stop talking and do something *real*." We understood this to mean: Let's actually implement and demonstrate, at least on a small scale, what we've been talking about.

You and Milenko, quoting Findhorn's dynamic founder, Peter Caddy, were now pushing Lisa and me and others. "IT'S TIME TO SOUND THE NOTE!" you said.

For some time we'd already begun talking "community." In 1977 several of us had met with an attorney friend to outline how an alternative community in Wisconsin might be structured. We drafted articles of incorporation and received non-profit status for the High Wind Association, Inc. Its principal purposes: to develop a sharing community where people live together in cooperation with one another and nature; to design and build shelters and power systems and small enterprises that use renewable energy and ecological systems; to work sensitively with the land as a cooperative enterprise with nature; to recognize chemical-free agriculture as a natural activity of human community; to serve as a demonstration in living and working consciously; and to play an educational role in generating and disseminating knowledge gleaned from our experience.

We also wrote a High Wind credo, authored primarily by Lisa, which, to our satisfaction, has remained relevant over the decades:

> *To walk gently on the Earth,*
> *To know the spirit within,*
> *To hear our fellow beings,*
> *To invoke the light of wisdom, and*
> *To build the future now.*

Since Lisa and I owned a small 46-acre farm 50 miles north of Milwaukee, we decided to dedicate its use as an experimental worksite and for possibly creating a modest community. With the existence of an organization and a specific physical site, all the human energy that had been bottled up was let loose—almost like a rocket. Volunteers from the Milwaukee area and elsewhere joined forces to spend each weekend renovating the crumbling farm buildings. We cleaned out the chicken poop to turn the old coop into a post and beam hostel where people could stay. We brought water and a septic system into the turn-of-the century farmhouse for the first time, updated the kitchen, and built a bathroom to supplement the outhouse under the apple tree. To the south-facing side of the house we attached a funky little solar greenhouse for heat and vegetable production. The huge barn, formerly housing cows and storing hay, was rehabilitated as a place for programs and living space.

In 1980 architect David Bergmark, who had designed New Alchemy's bioshelters, counseled us in drawing up a small grant proposal for the U.S. Department of Energy to build our own bioshelter at High Wind. The grant immediately stimulated a nucleus of volunteers with a variety of skills to give up their jobs to form a construction gang. The farmhouse turned into what became known as the "pressure cooker." Its six bedrooms were quickly spoken for, and then latecomers carved out sleeping space in the barn and chicken house (now known as "Coop de Ville"). Carpenter Jim Priest was foreman at the bioshelter site. David Lagerman went half time as editorial librarian at the *Milwaukee Journal* to become our technical coordinator. Betsy Abert, who taught disabled kids, quit her job in spring to join us and cultivate a large garden to feed everyone. A short time later, Alida Sherman, a Ph.D. psychologist from a northern Chicago suburb, met us at a "transformation" workshop we presented and arrived at the farm to take over the kitchen. John Smithson, who had taught survival training in the Air Force, with his wife Cindy and two young daughters, took on responsibility for logistic jobs. Todd Broadie and Cindy Moran, former students of esoterics in Madison, were more interested in intellectual activities than physical labor, but were fascinated by the dynamics of the community and with you in particular. And so it went.

After a few months, the nucleus of the construction group decided they didn't want to return to their old jobs, staying on as charter members of the new intentional community. At the height of High Wind activity, the community numbered some 25 residents, including children. They were all volunteers, relying for subsistence on personal nest eggs or finding part-time outside jobs. When we generated income from programs, we'd share dividends.

You and I have shared a lot of varied teaching adventures and related projects. But I've always felt that the central role you played here, along with Milenko, was to collaborate with our courageous Wisconsin contingent in creating High Wind. While Lisa was our original visionary who planted the seeds, our intentional community mobilized a lot of folks to actualize our experiment. Its goals, like those of Findhorn and other communities, were ambitious. We were ordinary people, but with an extraordinary mission. We had started out tentatively, uncertain that we'd be able to stand up to our surrounding, sometimes hostile status quo environment. Could we ourselves—flawed human beings often disagreeing on how to proceed and sometimes finding it difficult to mesh our diverse personalities—really offer a credible alternative to the larger society? Your nurturing helped to make us think we had something to offer about birthing significant cultural change. I for one often sensed that there must be anomalous forces at work. There were the unexplainable insights that popped out from some depth within us that defied logic. I saw myself as a social scientist trained to respect reason, yet I and others were experiencing impulses and circumstances that seemed to defy reason and made us believe in our own individual and collective potential. There were energies that coalesced mysteriously from outside the accepted boundaries of the "here and now" world—perhaps gifts from Spirit. I had learned way back when working in the dire conditions of war-destroyed postwar Europe that solutions, even with the best political, social and economic methods and strategies, went only so far. Sometimes solutions were "impossible" until the intangible "Factor X" (Findhorn jargon) entered in.

Suddenly the farm became a collection of heterogeneous individuals living together on the land. With minimal planning, an organic process had been set in motion, which created a fledgling community. While Lisa and I kept one room in the farmhouse for our weekends there, the other five bedrooms were quickly occupied. When guests and other volunteers arrived they slept in the barn or pitched tents. Jim and David built a two-cubicle outdoor shower with water piped in from the farmhouse and heated with solar panels. Sometimes we staged events with 50 or more people, plus the residents, Since no one was paid, residents covered their food and utilities, while Lisa and I subsidized renovating the buildings and paid property taxes. The residents set up a rota for their cooking, and the kitchen soon became the center of activity and socializing.

While the big project at this time was to construct the bioshelter, following the specifications of the New Alchemy Institute, there were also other building projects. The residents were clearly a construction gang and the "community" just suddenly "sprouted up." Since initially minimal thought had been invested in governance and decision-making, fortunately, momentarily, it all more or less fell into place. Jim, with major assistance from David, clearly had the technical skills as construction foreman. Since Lisa and I had cultivated a half-acre tract for vegetables before there was any High Wind, Betsy rapidly created an impressive food production operation, pulling in plenty of volunteer labor both from on-site and from the city. The first year, Alida showed amazing talent for organizing the household and kitchen, and John Smithson led teams to get the barn and other facilities in shape for events. When a check had to be written, Lisa and I stepped in. The word soon got out about this unusual experiment, the news circulating widely through our educational programs and the early fascination of the media. The public was showing up in droves, providing more volunteers, small monetary contributions, and a steady influx of new residents. Lisa and I developed an incredible inventory of contacts, which had begun with the 1,200 people who attended the Caddys' talk in 1977 and continued with the many presentations by you and Milenko and all of us.

You, Milenko and your fellow Lorians were critically important during those first years in laying the groundwork for our continuing educational programs and public visibility. You folks were the magnet that almost magically created an atmosphere that took the New Age from the realm of mythology to a flesh-and-blood reality. All the new learning taking place was now being grounded in the High Wind community.

The first serious test of decision-making involved construction of the bioshelter. I won't get into the technical details, but the tension almost blew the community apart. Some of the difficulty was a gender chasm—the men versus the women. Eventually, the situation was resolved, but the women weren't happy. After this, we worked hard to make every decision by consensus with all the residents, and we resolved to be more sensitive to each other's feelings. Later on, as this process became unwieldy—sometimes occupying a whole weekend—we created a board of directors, which included several very active High Wind associates from outside the community, along with residents. I admit that I took major responsibility for doing this, pushed by you Lorians and others while initially the idea was opposed by several residents. Over the years the board became increasingly important and continues on today, still with four original members—David Lagerman, Barbara Prendergast, Lisa and me.

Gradually we realized that the community (as society-at-large) was like an orchestra: each person with unique individual talents, and given our non-hierarchical framework, reluctant to designate any one person as "conductor." We found the art of community, when it "worked," was to sand down our individual rough edges just enough to facilitate harmony, without smoothing out all the rich individual gifts and contributions. Now and then various residents, especially Joann Martens, provided an essential "glue" that creatively melded the commonly held "big picture" agreements about the High Wind vision and values while translating this into practical productive action.

At the time of High Wind's inception, the original group that bonded together to create the intentional community shared what we felt was the essence of High Wind. This understanding grew out of the exploration of ideas in our classes, and with you and Milenko and the Findhorn folks, and through our direct personal experiences of living and working together.

Soon, we were drawing in new people who were inspired by our vision, but they lacked those early influences and bonding. At almost every community meeting they raised the question: What is High Wind, really? What is its purpose? They became impatient with long, unproductive meetings where we decided everything by consensus; they pushed for more "efficiency." Lisa and I found ourselves facing "Founders' Malaise." While it was acknowledged that we had initiated the enterprise and had contributed heavily, what should our role be now? Everyone agreed that dealing with fundamental cultural change was complicated, but nevertheless they came with the firm expectation that it would happen. They brought their own personal visions of what an intentional community should be about. Communitarians were supposed to embody a special wisdom, and to exemplify ways of functioning that were different from "out there." But what about the economic issue—could they really be expected to work forever as volunteers, even with the high-minded goal of changing the world? When we asked advice from you and Milenko, you quoted Findhorn's Peter Caddy: Constructive discussion is always the first step, but at some point the best choice may be to invite those who become frustrated, or whose agendas turn out to be very different, to leave High Wind and start their own project.

Members of our group had periodic chats with your "very wise, experienced, and very loving presence" called "John" (a quote from your book, *Apprenticed to Spirit*). At High Wind we referred to this transpersonal collaborator as "Upstairs John." Initially I was skeptical about your John phenomenon until I became convinced that John was in fact bringing in new information. This happened when you invited me to a "John session" to discuss the state of the world at the height of the Cold War. I asked him whether a nuclear blowout was imminent, and posed political science-type questions that required technical responses that I felt were outside your area of familiarity. On a number of occasions you and your perceptive partner, Myrtle, arranged for John sessions with us at High Wind. We received specific and helpful insights in dealing with complex challenges of the community. Several times when we faced some turmoil, we found much help in these conversations that brought us significant information from "other dimensions" (whatever these were).

In my own case, I soon found I had two more or less full time jobs: continuing as chair of my University Extension department, Center for Urban Community Development, and teaching on campus—as well as serving, along with Lisa, as overall coordinator at High Wind.

I was finding considerable university support in linking my ongoing political science and urban work with the alternative thinking embodied in the new courses we were offering. A number of university officials and colleagues appeared open to the need to re-examine cultural values and institutions and conventional lifestyles, and some participated in our programs as attendees or presenters. My dean checked with the university lawyer for assurance that I could organize university cosponsored educational programs at High Wind on a property still owned by Lisa and me, so long as we received no personal monetary benefit. (Lisa and I financed High Wind heavily and donated land.) I also found ways for the university to pay you and Milenko as ad hoc faculty.

The three of us—you, Milenko and I—continued to churn out classes, usually jointly sponsored by the university and High Wind. We invited well-known resource leaders from across the country to come in as a kind of roving faculty committed to alternative thinking. In naming our courses we tried to avoid terms like New Age, substituting more "acceptable" traditional academic vocabulary, such as "transformation" and "paradigm shift." One popular semester-long seminar was "A University for the Future," which looked at new knowledge and skills that would be essential for survival into the future. Our thrust was exploring new thinking and creating models for institutions of learning that would be relevant for the different times we seemed to be moving into. During the semester we hosted a weekend think tank with a small invited group that drew up an outline for a future university curriculum. We came up with five kinds of questions related to world order, spiritual order, social order, material survival, and knowledge frontiers.

Sometimes our offerings remained non-credit. For example, you and Milenko led an 8-week seminar, "Quest for Wholeness," which drew a sizable crowd. Your goal was to look at ways to heal the turmoil and confrontations in our fragmented world and lives. Another popular offering was a 6-week series of weekend workshops with talks and models for practical application. They included well-known Iroquois leader, Oren Lyons, who revealed how the tribes picked an enlightened chief. George Ramsey, an architect from Georgia Tech, came to lay out his plans for a pedestrian solar village. Robert and Diane Gilman came from the state of Washington to stay a while to demonstrate "Living Lightly" (subsisting on raw foods and making their clothes of wool woven from sheep they raised). We brought Mark Satin, co-organizer of the New World Alliance, to speak about forming a national group to push for an alternative political system. Barbara Marx Hubbard, cofounder of the Committee for the Future, came to share her ideas on how to think as a futurist.

Since these diverse future-oriented events transcended traditional subjects and departments and disciplines, and were generating enthusiastic evaluations, I discussed with university colleagues the creation of a futures studies major or a futures institute. We'd pull together all this activity under one umbrella, as some universities were trying to do. There was considerable interest and encouragement for pursuing such "alternative thinking" initiatives, but it was not easy to penetrate staid university structures. And since we had already found ways to offer our courses, get them in the catalogs, and receive academic credit, there was another obvious route to consider.

This was stimulated by Lisa's and my participation in the first global conference of the World Future Society, held in Toronto in 1980. It was a mind-blowing experience. Virtually every noted futurist thinker in the world attended. At the outset, a panel that stole the show was a debate between a senior conservative futurist, Herman Kahn, and a brilliant young alternative economist, Hazel Henderson, with whom we later had considerable contact. While I participated in two panels dealing with alternative education, my priority was to identify other universities where colleagues were designing courses with quality and rigor that didn't fit into conventional curricula. Everyone seemed to agree that rather than working for structural change in existing higher education, the more realistic approach was simply to create pockets of creative pioneer thinkers and teachers within academia. If our over-arching theme was alternative thinking, an appropriate label was Futures Studies. This had an academic ring that people could buy into, it crossed subject matter boundaries, and most folks were interested in where society was going.

David, you remember that even before we met, you were dabbling with ideas about what a New Age curriculum might look like. My speculation is that had you remained in Wisconsin longer, we might have found a way to mesh our respective ideas even more than we actually did. Although you had no Ph.D. (not even a B.A), you were certainly an absolutely unique resource with no duplicate in our institution. As I reviewed your proposed curriculum, I knew we'd need to find the right terminology to pass university muster—if we were to sell it to UWM.

You shared your 14-page draft, divided into five separate areas. Each outlined a course in surprising detail, which I found very exciting. While the plan dealt with most of the same themes we'd been focusing on, it was more tightly put together than our eclectic offerings. You listed your general course subjects:

1. An Overview of the New Age as an Archetype of Transformation;
2. Holism and the Gaian Perspective;
3. The Paranormal;
4. The Transformational Paradigm;
5. Theology and the New Age.

We could envisage offering a similar series of courses to the High Wind residential community and others closely associated with us. Simultaneously we'd plan to use as much as possible whatever we were learning in the community's actual daily life. I doubted that any intentional community anywhere had organized this combination of rigorous intellectual activity with a commitment to evolve a real world New Age model. I was aware that Findhorn and other communities had periodic internal conferences and assessment exercises, but nothing quite comparable to the intellectual sophistication of your courses, along with a community commitment to translate the theories into practice. I could imagine university credit for the whole package—coursework *and* "fieldwork."

In our work together we did present much of what you intended in your model, but our offerings were not a well-integrated curriculum like yours, even though the totality had considerable similarity. Every summer for more than 10 years you and Milenko, and other Lorian colleagues joined us in teaching a seminar at High Wind. The university cosponsored these, and all our community residents participated; they were the highlight of our year. Burning issues the community was facing in its daily living were often integrated into the intellectual discussions.

Our best example of combining serious content with actual living was our series of semester-long offerings known as the "Three Community Living/Learning Seminars." Cosponsored by the university and High Wind and the other participating communities, students were drawn nationally as well as locally. Most enrolled for 12 undergraduate credits, or six graduate credits. The subject matter melded the philosophical/spiritual values of community life within the larger context of a commitment to act in bringing about cultural "transformative change." The format had participants living for one month at High Wind and in two other intentional communities. They participated fully in the life of each community. Mornings were dedicated to intellectual exploration, afternoons to various work activities, and evenings to general sharing and assessment of how everyone was doing. The students practiced forming their own small group/community and functioning with openness, honesty, and mutual support—while also interacting within the context of their larger host communities. They focused on the issues both groups were dealing with. We sponsored this course five times, until the international segments became too costly. Evaluations indicated that most of the total of 75 participants came back with life-changing experiences.

The first of these seminars was in fall 1984, a pioneering effort with 12 students testing the model. The first month was at High Wind, the second at the Sirius community in Massachusetts, and the third at Findhorn. In subsequent seminars we also went to Eourres, a farming community in the French Alps. A High Wind member was picked to lead each trip, while each of the three communities selected its own liaison faculty to work with the visitors. In 1984 at High Wind you lectured and led discussions for the first week, Milenko took the second week, ethnobotanist Lee Olson the third week, and I wound up the fourth week. While there were no exams as in typical university courses, students kept a daily log, and at the seminar's end wrote a comprehensive paper to integrate the total learning experience—also incorporating relevant readings and documents. We heard that other universities and communities were soon emulating our model.

David, as a base for your New Age curriculum, you imagined establishing an Institute that "would offer conceptual and practical skills to support individuals in their personal and collective efforts to cocreate a holistic planetary culture." Quite a challenge! As a pilot effort, you would invite five groups already working independently, to communicate with each other. You had in mind Findhorn in Scotland, the Chinook Learning Community near Seattle, High Wind in Wisconsin, the International Committee for the Future in Washington D.C., and your own Lorian Association made up of ex-Findhorn members now in the United States and Canada. Through sharing their visions and experiences they could begin to play the role of a "University for the Future without Walls." Another title you considered was an "Institute for Holistic Studies." I understand that while you found interest among these groups, your efforts were never implemented.

One New Age-type initiative that was partially implemented was the New World Alliance. You know its story. Mark Satin was a young draft resister during the Vietnam War who spent eight years in Canada. In 1978 he published a book, *New Age Politics*, an early attempt to articulate a new kind of politics, neither of the left nor right but suggesting a new way of looking at political systems. In the first year he sold 10,000 copies, and I used the book in classes. On returning to the United States he traversed the nation by bus, seeking out social change thinkers, editors, and leaders of groups in the remote backcountry. He sent out a 23-page survey to 500 people with multiple-choice questions, and got back 337 completed questionnaires. The responses, he said, "constitute a virtual treasure trove of New Age thinking." With Mark, a dedicated group founded the Alliance, a new political organization based in Washington. It began with 100 founding members. They published an amazingly comprehensive 98-page platform. In the Introduction he said: "This just begins a reconceptualization or paradigm shift regarding the very nature of politics. Equally important political work takes place in the community, the workplace, and in personal development and interpersonal relationships...."

I first met Mark at the 1980 Toronto futures conference where we served on a panel, and over the next couple of decades we got together periodically. Often when in D.C. on university business I'd stop to see him, he being the one paid Alliance staff member, in his bare-bones basement office. He edited a widely circulated newsletter, *New Options*, from 1984 to 1992, and later he reformulated it as *Radical Middle* in the years 1999 to 2009. This publication, while operating on a shoestring budget, had surprising influence, including with folks in government. I knew that you, David, sometimes saw him at conferences, and recently you wrote the foreword for the fourth edition of his *New Age Politics*.

At the end of the 1970s and in the presidential election year of 1980, there was a flurry of New Age ferment in our area of Wisconsin. You and Milenko and your Lorian collaborators were always a magnet for drawing in crowds. Our string of classes and other events excited more and more people "to want more." The New Dimensions in Governance seminar galvanized interest in a new kind of political thinking that would link vision and conscious leadership with political action. Not long after Mark's book came out, we invited him to Milwaukee to give a well-attended talk. He was a bundle of energy with contagious ideas heralding a new way to think about politics. He stayed with us and—always a dreamy sort—never noticed when his wallet ended up with his laundry in Lisa's wash machine. He agreed that the new High Wind community and our Milwaukee orbit constituted an ideal setting for trying to put into practice some of the abstract ideas of the New World Alliance.

The Alliance had pulled together some of the most astute, idealistic and politically sophisticated young leaders anywhere. Two key members of their board, futurists Clem Bezold and Bob Olson, spoke with me of their interest in organizing a national consultation to further explore their ideas. When they heard that you were teaching with me and consulting with the High Wind community, they pushed the idea of staging a national event in Wisconsin. I got the university to co-host this gathering in a Milwaukee mansion overlooking Lake Michigan. Two of the Alliance's well-known elected officials, progressive Democratic legislator, John Vasconcellos, of California and conservative legislator Miller Hudson of Colorado, sent out the invitations. Thirty-five attended, including eight elected Wisconsin officials. The weekend produced plenty of animated discussion on how to move the tired political world toward new modes of thinking.

Nevertheless, the New Age big-picture visionaries were constantly challenged by the elected politicians; they kept going back to focusing on their "Monday morning agendas."

How do we translate, they kept asking, your lofty aims to serve the planet when we arrive at work on Monday morning and have to decide how much to spend on unemployment issues? They did agree on the high-priority importance of continuing the dialogue. We got a lot of positive feedback on your role in bringing transformational thinking into policy-making.

To follow up after the consultation, I organized an eight-week seminar on transformation-oriented politics. Cosponsored by the university, New World Alliance, Lorian Association and High Wind, its purpose was to explore "how to interrelate practical politics, transformational political education, and the role of the human spirit in fundamental change." The faculty consisted of you, Milenko and me working alongside two of the most interested Wisconsin elected officials from the consultation—county supervisors Jim Krivitz and Dorothy Dean. This turned out to be a fascinating opportunity for you and Milenko to explore in some depth such topics as the relationship between transforming ourselves and transforming the political system.

At about this time the Alliance office in Washington urged us to establish in Milwaukee one of its first chapters in the country. Fifty people attended our initial meeting. A dedicated volunteer, Mary Kopac, agreed to coordinate, and Jim Krivitz was to play an ongoing creative role. The group met for several years, with some members supporting political candidates and attending hearings of official agencies. Some of the participants got involved as activists on the front lines, others were more interested in the intellectual dimensions, and a number became personally committed to High Wind. I felt responsibility to keep all of these activities we cosponsored in the orbit of "education," since my university department had to refrain from direct political activity.

We had reached a break-through moment in bringing this new thrust of alternative thinking to the attention of more and more colleagues and administrators. I knew one "tried and true" activity that university officials loved was putting on conferences. By drawing in leading thinkers and doers from varied backgrounds, this could fulfill the three essential functions of higher education. Exploring new intellectual ground contributed to the *research* role. Delivering significant knowledge and information fulfilled the *teaching* role. Offering practical experience and problem-solving models became the *service* role. Also, university officials selected by the conference welcomed the chance to participate in the planning function and to be given visible opportunities to make presentations. In addition, if the event generated income through registration fees, this was welcome "gravy." We were aware that to be a true "winner," the conference had to be well organized, with a timely, exciting overall theme. For those of us planning and running the conference, which included you, David, and your Lorians, as well as my department, the conference was an excellent vehicle for introducing new thinking on the alternative world into the cultural mainstream.

While my department, Center for Urban Community Development (CUCD), played a lead role, we pulled in many cosponsors. We put on two big conferences at the end of the 1970s while you and Milenko were still in the area. The first one focused on the Midwest region—we called it "People, Neighborhoods & Appropriate Technology: Tools for Building Community Self-Reliance." I was beginning to figure out how to interrelate our CUCD's traditional emphasis on urban poverty and racism with the alternative efforts we had been mounting with you and others. The focus of this conference was building community, a subject equally relevant to both worlds. We planned it so that talks and discussions would follow two tracks. Attendees could choose one or both, and we found most folks had a hard time choosing. One track dealt with the most creative problem-solving efforts in *mainstream* experience concerning urban issues. We opened with a keynote speaker from Washington, Robert Embry, a high official with the U.S. Department of Housing and Urban Development (HUD). Presentations dealt with new trends and innovative projects, and included my former favorite dean, Glen Pulver, now a University of Wisconsin professor and president of the national Community Development Society.

The second track recognized that even the best ideas and models of Track One were not adequate. Entirely fresh thinking was required, which could be considered *New Age Alternatives*. The keynote speaker was William Irwin Thompson, writer, historian, and former MIT professor, knowledgeable about Findhorn and new ways of thinking about larger societal trends, including imagining the planetary village of the future. Presentations included experimental work with energy conservation and renewable energy (e.g. the New Alchemy Institute's Ark), as well as holistic approaches to health, urban food production with sustainable agriculture, and neighborhood housing upgrades with appropriate technology. Your Lorian group described lifestyles that focused on the potential for caring, interdependent relationships among people and with the environment.

A year later, in 1980, we organized another weekend conference, this time national in scope. It pulled together a dizzying array of major thinkers from around the country. We called it "Transformation: New Dimensions of Growth for the 1980s and Beyond." Most presenters recognized that through the next decades, while our country and the world will experience rapid and dynamic economic growth, we must simultaneously begin to prepare for a world in a period of great change. The fundamental changes projected at the end of the 1970s and early 1980s were at the time critically important, but now as we look back, they barely took into account one of today's most ominous challenges—climate change. For me personally this was a rare moment to see in one place such a galaxy of wise, visionary resources. Although our planning budget for the conference was modest, we found that most presenters accepted our invitation to participate for minimal compensation. Everyone felt that *this subject was of earth-shaking significance.*

After our university chancellor opened the meetings, one of our first speakers, eminent futurist Willis Harman, began: "The United States and other industrial nations now face a series of dilemmas that may be insoluble except by a sweeping transformation of their societies...." Ervin Laszlo, renowned social scientist and research director at the United Nations, observed: "We are poised on the edge of another historical leap. Let us not lack confidence in our capacity for self-renewal. Now that we have been asked to build a new foundation, we should not hesitate to make it a truly new one."

As the breakfast speaker, one David Spangler challenged the audience: "The 1980s and beyond are a gateway. What lies beyond, whether of unfoldment or collapse, expansion or retreat, depends on how we direct our creative energies through that gateway as persons and as a species. Our values create the field that gives direction to our efforts. They are the lodestar for our journey into tomorrow. To liberate our future from the dangers of the present, we must look to what guides us and ensures that our values match the wholeness of our possibilities."

A leading industrialist, William Norris of the Control Data Corporation, gave a buoyant projection of our economic future but recognized that it would be folly not to comprehend the perils described by the others.

We could fill up this page with quotes from eminent energy thinker Amory Lovins, *Intensive Journal Workshop* founder Ira Progoff, alternative economist Gar Alperovitz, and on and on.

Not long after the conference, Harman called me from California. He said his friend, the governor of his state and Democratic Party presidential candidate, Jerry Brown, would be coming to Wisconsin for the state's 1980 primary. A long-shot victory here would be his last chance for the nomination. Since Harman was convinced that Brown, despite his negative press designation as "Governor Moonbeam," had the makings of a new kind of politician, he asked me to invite a cluster of influential Milwaukee area leaders to meet Brown. Jerry stayed at our house for two nights. The first night he gave a spectacular presentation to the 50 people we'd invited, including several of your Lorian group. We felt he truly embodied the image of an enlightened political leader, citing all the values and positions we'd been espousing.

Then the next day I followed him around to hear him deliver the standard tired party speeches to entirely different constituencies. There was nothing of what we'd heard the night before. When he returned that evening, we sat up late to hash over what had happened. Most of us understood he'd lose Wisconsin, but this was a great opportunity to present himself as a leader for the future. He said all his advisers told him he had to win Wisconsin, not project himself as a new kind of politician.

In November he was back in Milwaukee to give tepid support to Democratic winner Jimmy Carter. He told me he should have followed our argument; he realized he'd blown it. Twenty-four years later, in 2004, he wrote me that he remembered that second night's discussion. Today, many observers consider Brown one of the most enlightened leaders of the Democratic Party.

At around this same time I received a call from Maurice Aylward, a name you may remember since you became directly involved with him. He'd been a special agent with the FBI, as well as a business executive, and when he heard about our big Transformation conference, he was intrigued and contacted me. He brought what we all thought was a hilarious proposal. He told us that it's known that there are nuggets of hidden wisdom from ancient Egypt that would benefit our current society One of the great pharaohs, Ramses II (1304-1237 B.C.) had preserved a vial of his semen before his death, maintained sealed in a coffin within the bowels of a pyramid. There was also a stone tablet with a covenant declaring that one day a new pharaoh would appear, created from this semen, destined to contribute to resolving today's Middle East turmoil. All this was to be discovered by a renowned archeologist of our time. Maury was convinced that his made-up scenario would make for an earthshaking film that he'd produce. And since we were clearly deeply interested in "transformation," he was asking for our help. He said he'd cut us in with the first million dollars he'd earn from this lucrative project and would set up a foundation for "transformational education" that we'd run. You, being an avid science fiction aficionado and a skilled writer of same, agreed to draft the script. Your cliff-hanging drama had this famous contemporary archeologist arrange for his exceptional daughter to be impregnated with the ancient semen. The resulting offspring turned out to be a spiritually conscious, charismatic New Age-type leader who would be able to calm and heal the unrest among the Middle East countries. Since we all loved your script, Maury invited two New York screenwriters to fly out to Milwaukee. They got excited at the prospects, and Maury went to Paris where he lined up Omar Sharif to star in the film. Just as we were all primed to move ahead, Maury died. It had been a jolly romp—a welcome interlude in the midst of all the serious intensity we'd been dealing with. We agreed that you were a natural at applying your spiritual wisdom to a definitely far-out high adventure story!

A number of us frequently returned to a dialogue you and I initiated in the "New Dimensions in Governance" seminar: How to integrate the "priestly" and the "effectiveness" functions. In the fall of 1979—two years after our first contact and a year after we began our intense collaboration together—I scribbled some notes that emerged from our relationship. Now, as I was digging through old papers in preparation for writing this letter to you, I found a crumpled sheet scribbled almost 40 years ago:

> By "Priestly" we're referring to the overwhelming influence of love, of a Spirit-infused consciousness and purity, as the central motivating factor in human affairs. By "Effectiveness" we mean applying conscious behavior but in the context of confronting the everyday nitty-gritty details of fulfilling essential human needs—getting something done on the practical level. The priestly function requires constant reaffirmation and recommitment in order to withstand the pressures from an often-dismissive surrounding environment. The effectiveness function requires constant vigilance and sensitivity so that action is not sullied with unconscious behavior that imperils the sacredness of life.

In an environment that is basically ego-centered, materialistic and oriented to the short run, the priestly function is unlikely to be fully understood and accepted by the mainstream majority, although recognized and honored by the more consciously evolved. Those exercising the effectiveness function must deal with specifics and are constantly faced with the need to take stands. In a heterogeneous society where people have very different needs and interests, taking stands will create "counter stands" and conflict. The priest can and must provide clarity of vision and reaffirm faith in higher values. Without that spiritual source of wisdom and sustenance, the effectiveness-oriented person will be working in a values vacuum. But this person can collaborate closely with the "priest" in helping to provide outlets for the sacred qualities and assist in practical ways to implement the priestly qualities in specific settings within the surrounding non-holistic environment.

The two thus need each other. Without any practical outlets or connections, the priest can become a recluse or a visionary who is not taken seriously. He/she becomes simply an expounder of platitudes and empty rhetoric with little influence over others. On the other side, the effectiveness type can fall into activism without a clear purpose, can take on projects without quality, pursuing power or money or other vested interests only for their own sake. The two functions are complementary, yet it is doubtful that the same person can fulfill both functions in our present climate. The eventual long-term goal would be to create an environment where the two qualities are fully understood and accepted by each proponent—where they become integrated as a single large whole. In the meantime, each side has responsibility to recognize, accept, and work with the other toward that goal.

Without using any labels, in scribbling that piece years ago, there seemed a need and a hunger in both of us to create our rather unique relationship.

It's been 40 years since we met. A true New Age still eludes our civilization. We may even have lost ground. But hundreds, yes, thousands, have been touched by your presence. I'm convinced that many lives are not the same. Seeds of a new consciousness are planted all over. As I finish this letter to you, David, even a sometimes hard-headed skeptic like me knows that your influence and time with us have penetrated deeply into our Midwest soil.

The High Wind board: Bel Paulson, Lisa Paulson, Bob Pavlik,
David Lagerman, Barbara Prendergast, Maureen Gallagher (missing, Mel Blanke).

Professor Bob Pavlik embraces
planetary sustainability initiatives

Dear Bob,

It all began with a lunch. I figured this was another of my many encounters with someone who had heard about High Wind and wanted more details. You were highly recommended as a creative professor, a renaissance-type with myriad interests.

How could I have known back in 1992 that, as a fellow idealist and a very productive academic colleague, you would become a partner in helping to build a better world? Now it's been more than 25 years that we've been collaborating, and I've decided to write this letter to you to relive a few of our adventures together. These were not in the distant lands of Italy or remote Northeast Brazil but close by, in the labyrinth of higher education, and among people drawn by curiosity to the mysteries of intellectual frontiers.

I had recently returned from China and met with MPS (Milwaukee Public Schools) deputy superintendent Bob Jasna about the idea of preparing youth from the central city to be global citizens. In China I was invited to find American students to teach English to Chinese students. Jasna seemed enthusiastic about this prospect and urged me to meet Tom McGinnity, one of the most esteemed school principals in MPS. Tom wanted his students to participate, and knowing your eclectic interests, suggested that you contact me.

At lunch you wanted to learn about this China project, but especially about our High Wind community up in the rural countryside, with its multiple offshoots. One offshoot was the Plymouth Institute, a new organization we had just created to work on formulating a holistic think tank and other projects. I also mentioned that a number of us connected to High Wind were about to purchase a spectacular 144 acres contiguous to High Wind land to save it from commercial development, and that we planned to use it for ecological education. Before I continued with more, you realized that we shared a full plate of common interests, including the idea for a university seminar on Sustainable Futures I was about to offer. You wanted to attend.

I soon learned that you were one of the creative movers and shakers at Cardinal Stritch University, and a nationally known expert on Howard Gardner's theories about multiple intelligences. You were also one of the open-minded academics in the region exploring new thinking about the whole educational enterprise. In the coming years I was to find out that we shared the same understanding I'd had with David Spangler and a few others: that the deeper personal values had to be meshed with our intellectual and action efforts in order to produce maximum results.

My initial plan was to address this letter jointly to you and Wilfred Kraegel, who also became a close colleague. With both of you, I worked for years on the amorphous, complex life-and-death subject of building a sustainable world—the central theme of this letter. Since Wil died recently, and while you and I are still actively engaged, I decided to focus on my work with you.

First, though, I'll say a few words about Wil. We met initially when he introduced himself at the conference my university department organized in 1979: "People, Neighborhoods and Appropriate Technology." While he told me he was a senior actuary at Northwestern Mutual Life Insurance, his real heart was in futurism. He was the company's in-house futurist, which for that industry was a critical component. He was the best-known futurist in the Milwaukee area, and probably in Wisconsin, as well as being active nationally. We tapped him to play a significant role on the planning committees for the next two national conferences my department organized, as well as to participate in an array of other efforts. The most important of these was teaching seminars on sustainable futures for a decade with us at the university.

Before moving forward with this letter to you, Bob, I want to briefly review some essential historical background that you are very familiar with. It undergirds everything we're discussing and is the broad subject of this letter—promoting a sustainable world. In my view, next to the issues of war and peace, this is the single greatest challenge facing humanity.

In the early 1960s marine biologist Rachel Carson and other prophetic thinkers planted the seeds of the environmental movement. The term "sustainability" was just beginning to be mentioned in 1972 when the Club of Rome published its influential *The Limits to Growth*.

Sustainability really became recognized after the U.N. Secretary-General responded to mounting pressure to establish a World Commission on Environment and Development in 1983. *Our Common Future*, the Commission's important final report, was published in 1987.

The richer industrial nations had begun demanding action on the looming environmental crisis. The poorer countries were demanding that priority be given to economic opportunity, recognizing that half of the world's population was still barely subsisting on less than $2 a day. Since the Commission had to be aware that rapid economic growth was causing much of the environmental havoc, it had to find a formula to meet the critical needs of both richer and poorer constituencies. Thus, its agreed-on definition that combined environmental sustainability and economic development: *Sustainable Development is "development that meets the needs of the present without compromising the ability of future generations to meet their own needs."* It was said that to be truly sustainable, any action would have to take into account the "three E's"—Environment, Economy, and Equity.

Since this was all quite abstract, there was urgent need to ground the sweeping ideas into here and now reality. The U.N. Commission, with strong global support, organized what became known as the Earth Summit, held in Rio de Janeiro in 1992. It brought together thousands of citizens and world leaders to begin to design a broad action program. Called Agenda 21, this plan and initial strategy would seek a plan to achieve sustainable development in the 21st century.

Having been in Brazil 25 years earlier, I vaguely thought of joining the multitude, and, in fact, one good friend in Milwaukee, Nicki Johnson, did attend. On her return she was bursting with contagious excitement, never having seen such a concentration of dynamic human energy in one place.

When we began High Wind in the latter 1970s, our efforts, along with those at Findhorn and other intentional communities, were already focused in this direction, although "sustainability" was not yet part of the current vocabulary. The principal purpose of our founding documents included people living cooperatively together with one another and our natural surrounding environment. We would use renewable energy, sustainable agriculture, and other ecological systems, and would mount comprehensive demonstration and educational efforts that focused on living with a highly attuned ecological consciousness.

There were, of course, a thousand questions that quickly emerged from Rio that people like you and me and Wil, with so many others, were grappling with. I repeat that next to issues of war and peace, preserving the Earth's natural environment while also taking care of the essential needs of its people, was and is humanity's most essential challenge.

Many of these questions Wil and I addressed in our Sustainable Futures seminars that you participated in. Later, you served as one of our speakers, using multiple intelligences to rethink education. Over more than a decade, along with regular UWM students and some faculty and civic leaders, we reached hundreds of teachers and administrators from the Milwaukee Public Schools and other local educational institutions.

Here was the course format we used:

AN INVITATION TO RETHINK THE WAY WE SEE THE WORLD

In this day of tumultuous change, people continually ask: How can we think about and prepare for the future? Whether a teacher, a business or government or civic leader, a parent, or a student planning a career, we need to develop the capacity to look ahead. Moreover, the future doesn't just happen. Our actions or inaction today condition tomorrow's events. In a real sense, we do create the future.

During most of the past 50 years, much of the creative energy of America and the West went to responding to the challenges of the "Cold War." During the next 50 years, our most critical challenge may well be figuring out how to create a sustainable world. This will require our learning to rethink much of what we know and to cultivate values conducive to sustainable living. We will become ecologically literate, globally sensitive, technologically competent, and prepared to live in a diverse local and world community.

This is a core course in sustainable futures thinking. While we recognize that education is a chief means for identifying the knowledge and skills that we need, we're also aware that the whole educational enterprise itself is undergoing transformative changes. Thus this seminar focuses on helping us to rethink the future in the direction of creating sustainable lives and communities, while also fitting into and contributing to a context of ferment on how best to learn.

The course will culminate with class members building on the knowledge base of sustainable futures and transformative learning, to design a final project that is related in a practical way to their life or work.

SEMINAR SESSIONS

I. RETHINKING THE FUTURE

Sept. 8 Concept of seminar: relationship of futures studies to education and sustainable living.
Sept. 15 Understanding the future: core ideas, scenarios, forecasting.
Sept. 22 Paradigm shifts: changing thought patterns, whole-system thinking.

II. WORLDS OF THE FUTURE

Sept. 29 Demography: relating population to the Earth's carrying capacity.
Oct. 6 Ecology: interdependence of human and nature.
Oct. 10 Field trip to Plymouth Institute (10:00 a.m. – 4:00 p.m.)
Oct. 13 Gender: women's movements – how they are emerging and connecting.
Oct. 20 Technology: driving force of change.
Oct. 27 Governance and Economy: keys to global sustainable futures.
Nov. 3 Review of readings.

III. SUSTAINABLE FUTURES LEARNING

Nov. 10 Preparing for transformative changes in learning systems.
Nov. 17 Utilizing advanced brain-mind research. (Speaker: Robert Pavlik)
Nov. 24 Values for sustainable futures.

IV. SUSTAINABLE LIVING AND US

Dec. 1 Summary and class projects.
Dec. 8 Class projects

You and I participated in countless meetings encouraging people to rethink how they see the world and to think as futurists. To keep the complex issues as concise and understandable as possible, we mentioned five core ideas that futurists employ as they think about creating a more sustainable world:

- *Use of scenarios*: To identify alternative futures, we construct different possible futures, based on different assumptions and values;
- *Identifying long-term trends*: Each of us has a list of what we project as likely to happen, in 5 years, 25 and 50 years;
- *Transcending narrow fields and disciplines*: Since futurists look at all of reality, they are holistic thinkers, moving beyond a limited range of subject matter, nations and cultures, spanning time to include the past and present as well as the future;
- *Understanding paradigms, paradigm shifts, paradigm crises*: When people lose faith in accepted basic assumptions and ways of thinking, there is a paradigm crisis that ends in one of three ways: short-term reforms, postponement to

future generations, or alternative ideas that over time become a new dominant paradigm;

- *Applying the concept of transformation*: since "transformation" means moving form one state of being to another, this is used to describe *fundamental* shifts—fairly rare occurrences. The huge shift from today's culture to a truly more sustainable world would be genuine transformation.

In our animated Q and A discussions, participants were most interested in exploring how to make use of these futures-oriented ideas for practical action. For example, because the culture we live in is *not* sustainable, could they imagine what a sustainable world might look like? Regarding "imaging scenarios," we urged them to think of examples of practical alternative sustainable actions, even very small measures, for their own lives. Regarding "trends," we emphasized that our first responsibility is to educate ourselves with authoritative data on what is happening or likely to happen, given changing values and circumstances. Regarding "transcending narrow fields," those who have come this far will find themselves becoming holistic thinkers because they understand that the essence of reality is that everything is interrelated. Regarding "paradigms," people will begin to reconceptualize how they see the world, realizing that today's dominant paradigm is placing us in peril. There will be a historic cultural crisis because we are using up nature's capital that is basic to our livelihood.

You and I have invested hours on the subject of "transformation," recognizing that building a genuinely sustainable world will require truly fundamental shifts of our lifestyles and institutions. At some point we'll ask ourselves: What role as actors in this "revolution" will we play? How can we become a meaningful force for transformation? Will we be bystanders, hoping that a politician or someone else will take the critical steps? Or will we wait for a more enlightened future generation to offer leadership?

You flew with me to Washington to meet various agencies to gather the latest material coming out of the Rio Summit. This would enhance our teaching and enrich our already active sustainability-focused work through High Wind. We learned that President Clinton had just established the President's Council for Sustainable Development, a partnership of government, businesses and nongovernmental groups. One of its officials invited the two of us to sit down to learn about the Council, which was not a government agency but depended completely on the creativity of citizens and communities. Before we left D.C., we were invited to serve on the Council's Task Force on Public Linkage and Education.

You may remember that we shared a hotel room. Since we were still getting to know each other better, you were pummeling me with questions about the origins of High Wind. I told you about how Lisa and I met in the war ruins of Naples, our adventures in Italy, Brazil, and elsewhere, Lisa's first mesmerizing visit to Findhorn, the early memorable seminars with David Spangler, Milenko Matanovic, and others, and the amazing enthusiasm of a contingent of volunteers who gave up whatever they were doing to create the High Wind community. I shared with you the great possibilities that we—including a skeptic like me—envisioned, and also the struggles we faced when living in an intentional community that challenged so many conventional mores. I was impressed not only with your obvious interest, but also your understanding that the voyage we were on was not only resisted by much of the mainstream culture, but that the alternative world we were exploring was full of unknowns that would require teams of courageous pioneers.

Later, as members of the President's Council, we participated in the big national conference in Detroit that attracted an outpouring of interest in sustainability. In the workshop we presented on "Innovative Education," we described our efforts with High Wind and the public schools. Attendees urged us to package our experience for nation-wide application. One of my personal highlights was meeting Ray Anderson in the men's room. He was CEO of America's largest company manufacturing carpets, a high pollution industry. After he gave a fairly routine talk on environmental challenges, I told him that what the audience really wanted to hear was his own story of personal transformation. He had moved from being a conventional businessman to one of the business community's most visionary statesmen committed to sustainable development. By recycling old rugs to make a new product, he had created a small revolution in the industry. He replied, though, that it would be too embarrassing to tell his personal epiphany before thousands of people.

At home we were soon engrossed with a big decision. Should we buy the Silver Springs property? This meant taking on a major new project that could have significant ramifications for sustainable development in Wisconsin. We'd also have to accept considerable risk. I'm sure you agree it's a story not easy to forget.

You remember that Silver Springs was a 144-acre ecological treasure adjacent to our High Wind property, unique in the county for its special attributes. As the headwaters of the Onion River, two million gallons of pure water poured out of the ground every day through artesian wells and springs into a fish hatchery and 30 small ponds that in the past had made it one of Wisconsin's major trout farms. The property was also a luxury resort, with four comfortable two-bedroom chalets tucked into the edge of a thick pine forest on a high ridge. A part of this was a restaurant/conference center with seating for 70 with kitchen, dining room, and bar. An added advantage was proximity to the 15,000-acre Kettle Moraine State Forest. What disturbed us was that the businessman owner had now decided to subdivide this unique land into at least 25 building lots. For years we at High Wind had maneuvered to protect our pristine valley from commercial development and sprawl, so this was another call to arms.

While we came close to attracting various buyers with ecological values, each prospect fell through. The owner told us that he planned to put the property on the market by the end of 1992. Given its prime real estate quality, a rapid sale to a developer was practically assured. We then mustered a small group of High Wind friends and colleagues, all with an array of skills and backgrounds, to decide whether we ourselves should make an offer to buy, each of us accepting a financial obligation and sharing the down payment. You and I had just recently met, and suddenly you found yourself joining the group. Because the landowner liked our motives, which were non-commercial, he offered a donation of $100,000 if we'd make an equal down payment and contract the balance with a sizable bank loan.

Our planning group came up with an astonishingly creative array of ideas. We'd turn the property into an R & D center as a Midwest demonstration of sustainable development. With our several educators tied to universities, the conference center would be fully utilized. We'd designate a number of acres for a model ecovillage with intelligent land use, renewable energy for home construction, and a biological waste treatment system that used wetlands to purify the water—a system pioneered elsewhere in the country but relatively new to the Midwest. While 70 acres would be allocated for the ecovillage, each of the 15 units would have only a half-acre building area, while the balance of land would be held in common for use by all. A technology center would serve the community and also be available for people with at-home jobs. We'd hire minimal staff to manage the chalets and take care of fishermen coming for trout. We'd establish a non-profit corporation, Plymouth Institute, for the education and research components, and a for-profit company, Silver Springs of Plymouth, for the moneymaking enterprises. We named the overall project SpringLedge, which would be a close partner with High Wind, although separate legally and financially.

We had two outside allies who were egging us on, convinced of the project's significance as an ideal regional model for the President's Council. John Broomfield, a nationally known educator and civic leader, had received a grant from the Rockefeller Brothers to contact various "premier examples" of sustainability in America, and he spent several days with our planning group and also at High Wind. He was enthusiastic about this initiative and confident we'd obtain foundation support.

Our most ardent advocate was a dynamic black woman—Natalie Moorman, a civic leader in New York. A friend of David Spangler, I had met her at a couple of past events. Her interpretation of events usually had more ramifications than first met the eye, always ending with spiritual connections to guiding forces "Upstairs." She had an uncanny sense for calling us at critical moments. Whenever we wavered as to whether to "take the plunge," the phone would ring. Her bottom line was that Upstairs had ordained a number of centers to be set up across the United States with global responsibilities for ensuring a sustainable world, and we in Plymouth were being called to play a key role. I must admit that she was persuasive, especially because her focus was not primarily money or politics or education but the dictates and wisdom of "spirit." We were being called from another realm!

On December 30, 1992, our little group bought Silver Springs. Immediately, we adjourned from the bank to a local pub to try to swallow away the risky decision we'd just made. Lisa and I put up our house and other property as collateral for the $365,000 bank mortgage. You and I took responsibility to set up a national advisory committee of distinguished leaders, and in every instance people were eager to participate. The local press immediately made this major news, which continued for the next month. One long article was headlined: "High Wind to Expand, Buys Silver Springs Property." Its first paragraph: "A conference center, international think tank and an ecological research facility are only a few of the futuristic projects planned by the new owners. . . ." Articles in the *Milwaukee Journal* and *Chicago Tribune* discussed sustainability as it was beginning to be understood. A laudatory *Sheboygan Press* editorial concluded: "We don't know if the Institute can be economically viable. But all of us should be thankful for people who are willing to devote time, effort and money to learn how to develop technology that can peacefully co-exist with the environment."

Undoubtedly you recall the details, but I'll summarize briefly, and then will focus on points that directly involved you. One of our close collaborators, Bethe Hagens, an anthropologist from Governors State University in Illinois, designed a classy brochure that was an idealized version of what we'd been discussing. Her husband, Bil Becker, an industrial design professor at University of Illinois-Chicago, worked with me to establish four task forces to handle different aspects of the project, bringing together 40 people. Of particular importance, he recruited two eminent volunteers from Illinois: John Hinde, a creative water expert to figure how best to utilize the Silver Springs water; and Mike Gelick, a Chicago architect knowledgeable about solar construction. A young inventor, Jim Kennard, who had recently joined High Wind, began designing a prototype machine to convert organic wastes into fish foods, and a micro-hydro system. Our pro bono High Wind attorney, Mel Blanke, handled all the legal work and drew up by-laws for our two new corporations.

Quickly we found interest among educators who favored developing a core program to deal with concepts of living sustainably, as well as hands-on training and internships. You found your top administrators at Cardinal Stritch College interested in creating a regional learning center for sustainable development; this could relate to the new Ph.D. leadership degree at Stritch you were helping to organize.

You and Tom McGinnity, the creative principal at Grand Avenue Middle School in Milwaukee, and I consulted with MPS Superintendent Howard Fuller and school board president Mary Bills about organizing summits at Silver Springs with school principals and teachers. Since you had already developed an amazing network in the metropolitan Milwaukee area involving the best school staffs, you invited them to come out to the country for these popular weekends. The result was unexpected enthusiasm for envisaging new roles where schools would begin to integrate sustainability into curricula. Fuller decided to speak at our teacher summits (and, incidentally, he was ecstatic about the fresh trout dinners served at our restaurant).

Despite all these positive steps, our initial funding optimism turned sour. The early push by the U.N., by High Wind, and many others working on sustainability, had not yet penetrated the mainstream. While our own High Wind and SpringLedge efforts were attracting substantial news coverage, we found few donors ready to support the new initiative. In fact, we were getting desperate to come up with the monthly $3,200 interest payment, plus all the other costs. The workshops and tours were self-supporting, but they provided no margin for other expenses.

Luckily, at one critical meeting Tom McGinnity came up with a brilliant life-saving proposal. Why not use some of his federal money at Grand Avenue School earmarked for his 650 inner city students and 55 teachers? We'd offer a new kind of learning experience at Silver Springs/High Wind. Not knowing how his kids would respond, we designed a pilot test for fall 1993. A group of kids and teachers showed up and were introduced to everything we had to offer. It was a stunning success.

Our resulting proposal: a Milwaukee Public Schools Partnership with Plymouth Institute/ High Wind for Sustainable Futures. There would be four levels of participation: a one-day introductory program with 13 waves of 50 students and five teachers; then programs for two nights and three days with 40 students at a time and four teachers; then one week for 20 more advanced students and two teachers. Finally, if all went well, we'd offer a multi-year program with a career goal of entering a market that was opening up with jobs related to renewable energy and a range of related fields.

Since this was a unique proposal with a sizable budget, we needed the approval of Fuller and the school board. Even though he had spoken at the teacher summits and had heard about the student enthusiasm, he still had to buy into the new initiative. Your wife Sonja concocted a savory trout salad with all the trimmings for an informal lunch at his office. We billed it "out of the mainstream." This did it! He and the board agreed to go ahead, and the budget included money to build dormitory space in the High Wind barn for student and teacher sleeping accommodations. There were also dollars for program staff, and rental of facilities that we'd use for the monthly mortgage payment for almost two years. At Christmas time Tom wrote us a note: "What an exciting year this promises to be!"

You, Tom and I designed a basic three-day, two nights program—more or less integrated into the curriculum at Tom's Grand Avenue Middle School. Forty students split into groups of 10, each spending half a day of learning in four different activities: the adjacent Springdale organic farm, solar energy, aquaculture in our hatchery and fishing in one of the ponds, and introductory nature study. Some of the seventh and eighth grade fellows, almost fully grown and inner-city tough, held hands when walking through our woods, scared of the unfamiliar wildlife. Since at night there were no lights on the grounds other than the moon and stars, this darkness (not to mention spiders in the outhouse) was terrifying to kids accustomed to a noisy but unsafe urban environment. For most, this was a totally new experience.

Our inner city program, teacher summits and tours, and initiation of discussions about sustainability, were attracting a lot of visibility. Our friend Henry Halsted, vice president at the Johnson Foundation, imagined a day when Silver Springs/High Wind would create a world class international eco-conference center committed to new thinking about sustainability. This was enhanced in the summer of 1994 when John Broomfield sent us information on the Donald Reynolds Foundation, a new entity in Tulsa, Oklahoma. Since the

Foundation was providing substantial grants for new construction, I called the director and he said that funding for the conference idea Halsted had envisioned was exactly what they were looking for. He urged us to submit a proposal for 5 to 10 million dollars.

On a Sunday morning a number of us met at Silver Springs to picture what the new conference center would look like. Bethe Hagens had created a remarkable image. She began by describing "an ecological meeting place of exquisite integrating waterfalls and hanging gardens with fish and marine plants in a unique water/waste treatment system; overnight facilities terraced into the cliff for up to 150 guests built from natural, locally procured, non-toxic materials, all-solar; a green space dome for meetings. . . ." The hours melted away as architect Gelic sketched Bethe's image on his drawing pad; water expert Hinde figured out how the ponds and springs could be utilized; others fleshed out the center's other features. In mid-afternoon Lisa called—she was upset that her special celebratory Sunday dinner was getting cold and where were we? Then that night you invited Becker and me to your office in your suburban Milwaukee home. With you at your computer, we worked far into the night finishing a draft proposal. The foundation loved our first draft, but finally turned us down because they decided to limit early grants to only a few regional recipients.

We also hosted a two-day national conference, "Ecovillages and Neighborhoods," and the invited academics and practitioners told us that our ecovillage model was one of the most carefully thought-out examples they had ever encountered. The county and state planning departments were complimentary; this project would bring positive visibility to Wisconsin. John Todd, one of America's innovators in ecological design, spoke at a Silver Springs luncheon jointly sponsored with the local newspaper. He lauded our new waste treatment system pioneered by his New Alchemy Institute—called a "Living Machine." Bil Becker and I presented a workshop at the Midwest Renewable Energy Association where 125 people said they couldn't wait to visit. We had a number of buyers already making deposits to buy in.

On June 5, 1996, Mel Blanke formally conveyed a draft of the SpringLedge plan to the three-member local town board, also with documentation of support by state and county authorities. Two of us had met with the board chairman, a conservative but enlightened farmer who appeared open to approving our project. But the other two board members, representing the most vocal of the conservative local culture, were dead against us. We held additional standing-room-only meetings where we detailed the project, placing it in the broad context of thinking and acting sustainably. The local press tried to be objective, and basically favored the project.

Boiled down, there were four themes that killed us: our biological waste system, being completely new, was too scary, despite our data confirming its success elsewhere; our plan of home-owners owning some land in common was "communism" and alien to the local culture; our openness to "some affordable housing" that implied "urban encroachment, vandalism, and minorities"; and fear that our proposed small contingent of new home-owners would overwhelm the local culture and become an adverse political force. I'm sure this whole chapter is indelibly etched in your mind as it is in mine.

After the rejection, there was a plethora of articles published on how our work had stimulated the area to think about "smart growth." Editorials thanked us for our efforts. From *The Review* in Plymouth: "The SpringLedge proposal may well have served as a wakeup call to town officials and residents alike, warning that they could no longer afford to adopt a head-in-the-sand approach to development. . . ."

Soon afterward, we decided to design a mini eco-community, called Thistledown, for five buyers, copying many of the same SpringLedge ideas. With minimal discussion, the Town Board quickly gave its stamp of approval. But then we decided that for the time being it didn't feel right to disturb that wild field, and didn't go ahead with the new effort. (This was a part of the tract that Lisa and I later donated to the Buddhist Shambhala organization to spur the development of a major Windhorse Center.)

With sustainability-oriented thinking and alternative models in the air, you and I and several of us imagined that this might in some way impact our relationship to higher education. The UWM chancellor and deans had been actively involved in our events. I always arranged for some university administrator to participate in the conferences or workshops to introduce a speaker or offer a short keynote talk. You and I met a number of times with administrators and faculty at your Cardinal Stritch University, where ideas about collaboration with High Wind were explored. Your president suggested we approach the Johnson Foundation for a grant to fund new learning initiatives. Later, when you joined Marquette University, you linked into the beginnings of transformative thinking when organizing the Community Transformation program, with fellow professor and dean, Bob Deahl, with a large civic outreach of hundreds. You also played a key role when you joined distinguished professor Howard Fuller in the newly formed Institute for Transformation, with an array of innovative school efforts.

At various meetings with my chancellors and deans, I was sometimes surprised at their considerable amount of interest in our efforts. I was never clear whether this was merely personal curiosity about ideas and models that were outside of their usual mainstream orbit, or if they actually saw something that could have significant larger institutional relevance. Once UWM chancellor Joe Klotsche retired, he was helpful with us at High Wind. Most astute observers were generally aware that universities were quite desperate for new thinking. I was shown a trenchant private report about eight top administrators of major universities who were looking back on their struggles in the late '60s and '70s when they were facing the triggers of campus turmoil stimulated by the Vietnam war and the Civil Rights/black anger issue. With surprising candor, they concluded, "We were in over our heads." Today there was this seeming inability of the university and societal institutions generally to respond to the obsolescence of the surrounding culture.

I felt this momentum might become more tangible when our University Extension chancellor, Pat Boyle, decided to sponsor a three-day futures-oriented conference "to be in the forefront of examining the relevant, emerging issues. . . and determining their impact on the people of Wisconsin, the nation and the world." He established a seven-member planning committee that included two deans, several of his own staff, and me. It would pull in 150 representatives from the university's campuses around the state, along with civic leaders. Since no one else knew much about the futures field, the planning group continually turned to me to help design the program and identify speakers.

They used the two keynoters I recommended, whose works you and I both knew well. Mike Marien edited *Future Survey*, the monthly publication of the World Future Society, with dense abstracts of the best futures literature. There was nothing comparable in the world. He gave a withering critique of higher education and its lack of incorporation of futures thinking into its curriculum. His talk, "Universities in an Era of Multiple Transformations" (EMT), identified the ten most significant megatrends that every student should be prepared for. He said the University of Wisconsin could play a national leadership role with the "global *problematique*."

The second speaker, economist Hazel Henderson, wrote *Politics of the Solar Age*, a classic pioneering work that reconceptualized politics and economics toward an interdependent world. She emphasized that this would require a historic paradigm shift in western culture, and she was one of the first to challenge the corporate world to wake up in today's waning years of the petroleum age. Both speakers discussed the deficiencies of higher education and the huge opportunities for intellectual leadership. She too urged our University of Wisconsin to take a lead role. It's important to keep in mind that these talks were in the 1990s. Unhappily, we recognize that today, rather than moving forward since the enthusiastic vigor of events such as that conference, our politicians currently are going backward, and higher education, too, has been timid and unimaginative, failing to recognize the urgent societal need to begin to shift toward building a world that is truly sustainable going into the future.

The chancellor, in his closing remarks at the conference, was very supportive. He urged that "we continue this important dialogue, and the university has a role to play." He said he'd reconvene the planning committee to discuss possible future directions. This never happened. While we felt the conference was useful for the public visibility provided and planting a few seeds, we concluded that any action to move ahead would depend on individuals like ourselves, not the broad institutions.

As I participated in meetings such as this conference, I understood even more the unique qualities of people like you and our other colleagues. So much could be accomplished if there were many more of us: people with modest egos, who blew no horns but had advanced training and a limitless thirst to learn more. People who were aware of the complexity of what "sustainability" really required. The U.N. and the many new forces getting interested in an integrated approach that tackles all the connected issues of our civilization had to recognize that this was still largely a great unknown. Although our universities were presumably among society's most significant generators of knowledge, their energies thus far were only beginning to touch the subject. This was a terrific moment for idealistic pioneers, who—rather than being motivated by fame or power or money—were true explorers.

We had to start out by building on what we knew, then linking up with the best new ideas. Bob, you will remember one of the teacher summits we held bringing in national consultant John Cleveland from Michigan. With 70 carefully chosen, mostly inner city public school teachers, we spent the weekend exploring how to enrich what they were doing, all while placing their efforts in the context of building a sustainable society. Our topic on New Learning Theory and Practice we titled "Learning on the Edge of Chaos." Cleveland had been offering similar workshops around the country, and while he felt they were useful, there was something missing. He sensed a certain emptiness, that he was spinning his wheels. We expressed similar feelings.

It turned out that all three of us had been finding impressive insights in the writings of the penetrating thinker, Ken Wilber, a leading theoretician on the subject of consciousness. You remember his models that conceptualized the relationship between the personal inner self and the exterior world, summarized in his *A Brief History of Everything*. Wilber had first studied the physical sciences, then psychology and the social sciences, and then immersed himself in both Eastern and Western religions, ending up as a practicing Zen Buddhist. He traced the evolution of consciousness through history, viewing evolution not simply biologically but also as spirit in action. Like other spiritual philosophers we knew, such as David Spangler, he saw evolution as a process toward wholeness, both in one's own individual self-actualization and as part of the human story.

On the spot, the three of us agreed to organize a gathering at High Wind in October 1996. There would be no agenda, no speakers—just some fertile minds—to explore Wilber's thinking and its relevance to our own spiritual paths and work lives. We were thirsty to combine all the important intellectual content and discussion of failing systems of the educational establishment, with more focus on the values that motivated us.

You and I knew that the essence of our experience with High Wind was not primarily political or economic. High Wind was a community of consciousness. Now we had to find a way to tap into the wisdom and the intuitive inner voices within us and all the teachers and others we were working with. In our busy activities dealing with sustainability, where the documents we'd been using of the U.N., the Club of Rome, and others emphasized the admittedly critically important physical dimensions—conservation of natural resources, world economic development, renewable energy—we needed to place all of this into a *values* context.

At the High Wind gathering, we quickly zeroed in on Wilber's explanation of the stages of an individual's evolution of consciousness. He started out with our **Newborn** stage, and then to our **Emotional Self**—the beginnings of our capacity to think from ages one to three. And then on to the beginnings of our **Conceptual Self** from ages three to six—using symbols and language. In his view, by ages six to seven and into adolescence, we begin to form our individual **Role Self**. We take on tasks, recognize the rules of socially accepted behavior and conventions, and join groups from the immediately local to the national and beyond. We now have found an identity and joined the mainstream culture. Wilber is convinced that most people never evolve beyond this stage. The educational system and institutions prepare the population for this level.

Wilber then conceptualizes the next higher levels in his stages of conscious evolution. His term: **Worldcentric Self. Mature Ego** is where the capacity for global awareness emerges. We imagine different possible worlds, with the ability to stand outside and criticize the mainstream conventional culture. Next, we move into his sixth level: **Integrated Thinking**. Here we have the ability to integrate and synthesize, to combine inner and exterior awareness and the interconnections between the human and the natural worlds. He recognizes that this is difficult to achieve and few people do. Beyond this level in his typology, we move into the transpersonal realm: the psychic, soul development, pure spirit beyond self—**Non-duality** "isness."

In our animated discussion at the gathering most of us agreed that our work had been focusing too much on the exterior world. We were investing huge amounts of energy into pushing and shoving around all the forces *within* the mainstream conventional world, when in actuality we ourselves and our many compatriots were starved for breaking out of this deadly environment. We needed more inspiring values. We needed to refocus our initiatives in our roles as integrated thinkers, bringing together within ourselves and in our work both interior richness and external efficiency with systems and institutions.

You and I and others at High Wind, such as our long-time colleague David Lagerman, invested hours in figuring how to apply Wilber's "four quadrant" matrix to everyday use. Here is Wilber's map of reality, simply charted (see next page).

As we know, the right hand of the chart deals with the exterior world of empirically observed behavior, while the left side focuses on the interior world of values. The upper right and left quadrants focus on individuals, and the lower right and left quadrants deal with collective/societal realities. In our workshops with teachers and our courses on sustainability, we focused heavily on the intellectual dimension (upper right quadrant): amassing the essential knowledge needed for real school reform, and for advancing sustainability. Likewise, we grappled with mastering the technologies required (lower right quadrant) to translate what we know into tangible results, using whatever systems and institutions we find relevant.

But increasingly we found that these dimensions of the exterior world, important as they were, were not enough. Our goals were, in essence, radical. We had to push out of the

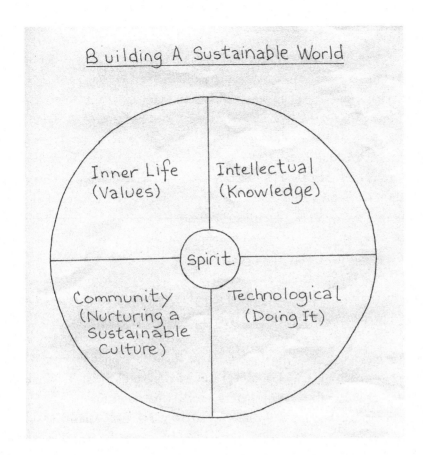

Building A Sustainable World

Inner Life (Values) · Intellectual (Knowledge) · spirit · Community (Nurturing a Sustainable Culture) · Technological (Doing It)

status quo. We had to take risks. We needed values that inspired us to take on big challenges, the inner strength and motivation to break out of mainstream dysfunctionalities that continued to lock us in. Our values as individuals (upper left quadrant) and of our broad culture (lower left quadrant) belong in the interior world. We knew our challenge was to prepare ourselves, and others we were working with, to integrate all four quadrants. As integrated thinkers, we could then see the world as whole systems. We could enable ourselves and our colleagues to function at higher levels of consciousness. Back when we were discussing with John Cleveland the missing ingredient of some of our professional activities, we realized that this Wilber-oriented gathering reignited the leadership roles we were meant to play. The gathering was so beneficial that we organized a second one, with even more folks, the following year.

You, Tom McGinnity, and I were asked to sit down with Howard Fuller. He had just resigned as Milwaukee Public Schools superintendent, after four innovative but frustrating years. As one of America's best known black activist educators, he was exploring what to do next—how best to utilize his talents. As three of his strong supporters and backyard confidants, we brought in another friend, Mary Bills, the most creative member of the MPS board. Keeping in mind our recent discussions to unite values and action, our small group soon agreed on the need to address these questions: What is most needed for education in Milwaukee? What is the vision and how could we make it happen?

Howard invited 100 local civic leaders to meet with us for four evenings to come up with answers. The sessions proved productive. A new Institute for the Transformation of Learning was established in 1995 at Marquette University, with Howard as director—Distinguished Marquette Professor. The Institute developed wide-ranging activities to support exemplary education options that transform learning for children. It focused on low income and minority students and the educational institutions needed. With his broad contacts, Fuller formed national groups and generated ample funds. He hired you as his chief assistant to run the operation. For 20 years your partnership with him has offered an incredible array of programs. You also collaborated with the visionary Marquette dean, Bob Deahl, to create the Center for Community Transformation, to build a sense of community in the fragmented Milwaukee metropolitan region.

You remember that at this time there was a lot of environmental interest in the air. The U.N.'s documents on sustainability were beginning to circulate. Word was coming back from the Earth Summit in Rio de Janeiro where thousands had come together from all over the world, to begin to formulate a sustainability agenda. I had recently returned from Shanghai, China, where I co-chaired an international conference on the relationship between environmental challenges and economic development. Wisconsin's Senator Gaylord Nelson had been pushing Earth Day ceremonies, and a number of organizations in Milwaukee, led by Mayor Norquist's wife, Susan Mudd, and environmental groups, including my university department, had formed the Milwaukee Coalition for Global Survival. All of this led to a well-organized event, the Environmental Town Meeting that attracted hundreds—politicians, business leaders, and church members. High Wind's Milwaukee bookstore had an on-site stall with 15 key books.

While we were tired after all the work for the Town Meeting, the Coalition kept asking, What next? The President's Council on Sustainable Development that recently had been established (and included you and me on its Education Task Force), kept pushing this theme: the U.N. and governments can pass resolutions but the real action will take place at the state and local level. After a year, several of us from the Coalition's steering committee volunteered to form a statewide steering group "to design a cluster of specific, doable, locally based strategies to promote sustainability." With minimal effort, we were surprised at how many folks we invited—legislators, mayors, university representatives, business and environmental organizations—wanted to join what became known as Sustainable Wisconsin.

This group soon had 20 bases of local activity around the state. Each base had a coordinator/convener, who served on our statewide steering group, and whose role was to relate to the governor's office, the legislature, and national sustainability groups. Sustainable Wisconsin sponsored a statewide conference at Stevens Point in the middle of the state. The 60 attendees designed a summary of goals for Wisconsin and found the enthusiasm to continue on. However, several of us admitted frustration when the governor's representative, who was very supportive, offered to establish an office for Sustainable Wisconsin in the capital—but the most vocal participants turned down the proposal because Wisconsin currently had a Republican governor. Instead, each local base decided to go its own way. Nevertheless, our efforts were recognized publicly as a local model by the President's Council on Sustainable Development.

Returning to Silver Springs, after the Mitchell Town Board rejected our ecovillage project, we were now seriously thinking of selling the property. Out of the blue I received a call from Joan Robertson, sister of our deceased old friend Roberta Klotsche (wife of UWM's chancellor Joe Klotsche). She'd consider giving us a challenge grant of $100,000 in order to advance our sustainability goals. This led to her hosting a luncheon at the exclusive Women's Club of Wisconsin in downtown Milwaukee. We assembled 20 key people in December 1998. You and I offered a plan for a "Center for Sustainable Living and Learning—Preparing Teachers, Leaders and Youth to Build a Sustainable World." You detailed the huge possibilities and there was a new burst of creative energy.

In short order you convened a meeting of 30 fairly high-powered people from various educational institutions. We posed this question: Given the perils we all know, can we take a lead in building a sustainable world within our own orbit of leadership? While those present were positive, the same old problem surfaced: how could we create constituencies in our educational institutions to invest resources when they are more part of the problem than the solution?

We pinned down the most interested among those present, along with a contingent of High Wind colleagues, to organize four task forces. The goal: to design a plan for a Sustainability Institute based at Silver Springs, in cooperation with various educational institutions. Keeping in mind Wilber's quadrants, the Spiritual Group agreed on the most essential values that would give heart to the project. The Intellectual Group centered on the building blocks required to truly understand sustainability. The Technology Group brimmed with ideas to demonstrate sustainable practices. The Community-building Group coalesced around what such a sustainable enclave would look like.

When the task forces convened for a weekend retreat in April, their reports were impressive. Then everyone turned to you and me to figure out the next steps. I must admit that after the enthusiastic energy that all of us had invested to think through and make the Spring-Ledge ecovillage real, and subsequently the disappointing turn-down by the town board, we felt very deflated and exhausted. Both you and I had fulltime, demanding university jobs. The bank that held the mortgage on Silver Springs required its substantial monthly payment and was nervous after the ecovillage was rejected.

When one of the wealthy Kohler family came forward and offered to buy Silver Springs, and then would transfer most of this beautiful real estate to the Wisconsin Department of Natural Resources as a wildlife preserve, you and I and the others who had been participating in this noble adventure agreed that despite Joan's challenge money, it was really time to sell. And so ended this unforgettable adventure!

You recall that in 1991 High Wind itself had changed its status from an intentional community to a less intensive Learning Center. For 10 more years we brought people from all over the country to its programs. But then, just as with the Silver Springs initiative, those of us who had been providing leadership for all this period were really burned out. Reluctantly, we decided we'd had enough. In 2001 our High Wind board agreed that if it could find compatible collaborators, we would consider selling the "campus" that we had used for so long. This included the bioshelter and adjoining land, and the farmhouse with its contiguous outbuildings, including the barn that had served so well for 30 years. In short order, two Buddhist groups that had been hosting retreats at High Wind in past years, stepped forward. We felt that they shared our outlook, which meshed spiritual values with concrete programs, and like us, they loved and revered the land. This whole story of the sale and letting go of our beloved buildings that you know well, has been detailed elsewhere.

Since all of us on the High Wind board were continually running into people who had participated in some way in our orbit of activity—not just community residents, but those involved with educational events, conferences, tours, the bookstore—we were curious. What influence had High Wind really had on these people's lives? We constructed a comprehensive questionnaire, truly formidable in length and complexity. We sent it to 180 folks on Lisa's shortened but still incredible mailing list. Respondents were told they could be anonymous so that we'd get authentic data, but everyone except one gave his or her name. We were impressed that 60 completed the survey, giving us a mountain of data.

You, Bob, volunteered to play the heroic role of analyzing all the material and providing the board with a thoughtful five-page summary. There were laudatory comments as well as critiques. In one question you showed how their association with High Wind had affected their choice of work, geographic location, house design and energy efficiency, family life, and philosophical beliefs. A frequent comment: *The mere fact that High Wind exists is important.* Despite its deficiencies, the paradigm it represented—challenging mainstream culture—had staying power. Responses to another question posed for folks who had actually lived at High Wind yielded even more valuable insights and evaluations. Lisa and I each responded in depth to the question: Would you live in a community again? Our responses were different, and I'll refer you to our respective books for our explanations (which you know well).

With the sale of the "campus" property, High Wind now had a small pool of funds, which over the years multiplied through careful investments in the stock market by board member

Mel Blanke and me. The High Wind Foundation now began providing small grants, using income from the principal, to worthy non-profits with a commitment to sustainability. A broad spectrum of grantees have benefitted. The board appointed you as executive director, and we've met several times a year to accept proposals and allocate resources annually to more or less a dozen grantees. We must reaffirm the terrific leadership you have provided in taking major responsibility in running the foundation.

I'll mention an unfolding project or situation that for the two of us has consumed considerable energy in recent years: first Windhorse, and then Glen Cairn. Since the two Buddhist groups made their purchases almost 20 years ago, we've had ample contact with Japanese Zen Buddhist, Richard Brandon, and his family who acquired the farmhouse property, and the Shambhala Buddhist group that bought the bioshelter and is now known as the Windhorse Retreat Center for Meditation, Peace, and Sustainability.

Richard died last year and his wife and one son and disparate supporters have used the property to mount occasional programs. Richard indicated that if and when the day comes that they decide to sell, the first option to buy would be offered to Windhorse.

It was in 2001 that the Shambhala Buddhist couple, Alan Anderson and Sue Firer, bought the bioshelter on behalf of Shambhala International. As you know, Lisa and I have had close ties with Alan and Sue over almost two decades, sharing with them our experiences with High Wind, and at one time stoking their interest in linking their Buddhist philosophy and practices with our spiritual background, educational programs and technological efforts with renewable energy and sustainable community. Given our likely positive future collaboration, Lisa and I donated some of our land to Shambhala, feeling that this organization could become a worthy successor. This was greatly enhanced by our conversations with various national Shambhala leaders who strongly endorsed this cooperation. They projected a significant future role for our cooperation beyond Wisconsin. The linkage with Shambhala has produced a number of excellent programs but also has had its ups and downs since Alan and Sue divorced five years ago. We've dealt with their several governing groups, with Sue taking on the director position several years ago. You and I have invested significant time in many discussions, both locally and nationally, with the Shambhala folks, with expectation of a fruitful future partnership.

A creative offshoot of our involvement with Windhorse is the Glen Cairn eco-community project. Four years ago Windhorse organized a regional meeting, "Touching the Earth," with some 80 people attending. One of Shambhala's international leaders, who has a job overseeing Canadian sustainability, played a central role. Various ideas for the Windhorse future emerged out of that weekend. One initiative that bore fruit was to build on High Wind's past experience to consider forming a small eco-community that would draw into the area additional creative energy and resources. You and your wife, Sonja, in a very generous move, agreed to sell 20 acres, adjacent to our collective properties, that you had owned for years. With your significant help, we enlisted the Town of Mitchell to rezone this special land, contiguous to the 15,000-acre Kettle Moraine State Forest, into four five-acre residential tracts. Our son Eric and his wife, Angelynn Brown, agreed to design and build a state-of-the-art net zero energy house on the first lot. Another chosen associate, Elizabeth Matson, acquired a second tract. This new enclave named the project Glen Cairn and recognized its close historic ties and spiritual affinity to both Findhorn and High Wind. It will serve as a valuable ally for whatever transpires as the future of High Wind and Windhorse unfolds.

I would be remiss not to emphasize that although High Wind's lifetime has evolved through many chapters, our commitment to build a sustainable world has never wavered. In fact, we've continued to deepen our understanding of the meaning of "sustainability." Since this term was popularized by the United Nations in the 1980s and 1990s, it has been worked over by thousands of organizations across the planet. Like so many originally meaningful terms, in some eyes it has now become something of an empty cliché. The early definition was spelled out in the U.N. book *Our Common Future*: we must work to fulfill today's needs without compromising the needs of future generations. This was followed with the detailed Agenda 21, decided on at the Rio conference in 1992, to preserve the world's natural resources, along with eliminating world poverty. These recommendations in turn were dramatically enhanced with a series of U.N. reports beginning in the 1980s on the perils facing the earth due to climate change.

Since much of this discussion and implementation of sustainability efforts focused on the physical and materialistic dimensions—in their own right obviously critically important—some of us renewed our earlier discussion on the relationship between the *exterior* and *interior* worlds—addressing the central importance of individuals' emotional status, values, and culture. We recognized that we were facing an ever more serious societal crisis, that sticking to the status quo or "business as usual" was not an option. We needed to rethink our lifestyles and institutions. Our original intention at High Wind—to "live lightly on the land" and to promote conscious sustainable community—is even more imperative today.

More and more we're finding people who sense the need to tackle the question: *What is a sustainable community?* The Earth's acceleration toward natural disaster is becoming ever more imminent to many of us. As our government and the populace at large have become submerged in mainly "here and now" priorities, we see that our original High Wind mission takes on even more urgency.

We inspire, assist, and modestly subsidize others who offer worthy creative efforts. Over the years our innumerable grantees fit into this category.

Looking back, you and I have continued to collaborate with others to frame pilot initiatives. For example, several years ago we identified 10 different essential facets of community life in Milwaukee, and planned the formation of 10 small perceptive teams to gather the best available information and insights to describe the characteristics that would make that sector "sustainable." The data would include both material/physical essentials and the deep-level values of the culture of that prospective area. The richest part of the project would be the final interaction of the teams—their collective definition of what "sustainable community" means for the Milwaukee environs. Then the project's conclusions would be shared with the city's decision-makers. This idea, along with others that remain on our drawing board, continues to stir us as we look to the future.

As I finish this letter, I'll mention that just a few days ago we convened one of our periodic "Mountaintop Conversations." These are occasions when you and I, and often Tom McGinnity, station ourselves away from telephones and all electronic devices to review "the big picture." We focus on significant ideas and events beyond today's operational details. For example, we recently lunched with eminent educator Howard Fuller who reassessed his influential work all over the country empowering minorities. He was asking himself: When is it time, if ever, to quit? We also talked with Bob Deahl, who after years of spiritual and academic leadership, has decided: I'm ready for a memoir. Later that day there was a nostalgic dinner with close former colleagues of CUCD, my old university department, who recalled amazing stories of folks we worked with who rose from nothing to distinguish themselves. We agreed that our "sweat and blood" toil together has been very worthwhile. Two days later we attended a reception with leaders from Youthaiti, a grassroots organization High Wind helps to fund, which created a Center for Sustainable Living and is building sanitary facilities in Haiti's worst hurricane-destroyed community. A couple of hours later we found ourselves at a rousing, cutting-edge live show arranged by our son, his wife, and their staff. They were focusing on the Future of Water, Milwaukee's precious and endangered Great Lakes resource. Steve and Anne are public radio producers reaching out nationally. In passing, at this Mountaintop sharing, I reported that Lisa and I have a newly born second great grandchild, Quinn Johanna Paulson. What kind of world is she entering? We hope, and have to assume, that it will be positive!

You and I know that all of these indicators, minuscule items in themselves, are fragments that together forge the big picture. And I believe it can be a bright future, **IF THE BEST HAPPENS.**

Made in the USA
Monee, IL
26 January 2021